MAMMAL DETECTIVE

MAMMAL DETECTIVE

• ROB STRACHAN •

with illustrations by the author

Whittet Books

First published 1995

Whittet Books Ltd, 18 Anley Road, London W14 OBY

British Library Cataloguing in Publication Data. A catalogue record for this book is available from the British Library.

ISBN 1 873580 20 7

Printed and bound by Biddles

Acknowledgments

If I attempted to list all those people who have influenced me or provided an opportunity to hone my 'detective' skills, it would go on for several pages and no doubt I would still have missed people out. However, a few names must be included as they are great mammal detectives in their respective fields and they have provided me with both inspiration and encouragement, either in person or through the books they have written. Firstly, I must mention Ernest Neal, the author of my first mammal book, *The Badger*, that whetted my appetite for more knowledge about all secretive mammals. Michael Clark's *Mammal Watching* carried that quest further by describing the best ways to 'find' different species but it also introduced me to the Mammal Society where I could glean from the experts, Pat Morris, Derek Yalden, Bob Stebbings, Stephen Harris and David Macdonald to name but a few.

Among my contemporaries I must also mention Johnny Birks, Phil Richardson, Arthur Rivett, Terry Coult and David Balharry, with whom I have not only been able to spend time out in the field but who were also able to provide some valuable comments on early drafts of this book.

Also I must certainly thank Paul Chanin and Don Jefferies for the faith they placed in me to be able to carry out almost continuous paid fieldwork on 'elusive' mammals since 1985 and to the Nature Conservancy Council (now English Nature) and the Vincent Wildlife Trust for funding the various projects and surveys.

I'm especially indebted to the Hon. Vincent Weir, who very generously met all the costs of the Water Vole Survey of England, Scotland and Wales and the Otter Survey of England. I'm also very grateful for the luxury of a brand new camper van that I made my mobile base for the surveys and became a way of life for five years – I miss it now it's gone.

Contents

Introduction

My passion for mammals stems from some of my earliest childhood memories; perhaps it all started during an encounter with two harvest mice that had found their way into the back garden rabbit hutch and were actually bold enough to take food out of my hands. Later, in the same year, I found an occupied dormouse nest in a local hedgerow, located a noctule bat roost in a tree hole and saw my first badger ambling across the road in the car headlights. By the age of ten I had discovered the delights of making casts of footprints with plaster of Paris and was on the road to becoming a mammal detective.

Many of Britain's mammals are shy, elusive or nocturnal (even all three) and are therefore difficult to observe. Field mammalogists, then, have to turn detective and enter a world based on visual clues, distinctive smells and occasional calls in order to find the identity of those mammals that are present but rarely seen.

This book has been produced to help piece together those clues aided by simple keys and illustrations. It is in part another field guide to mammal footprints and their droppings, but I hope you will discover that there is a lot more to mammal detection work than the simple identification of the various signs in front of you. My aim is to help you understand and interpret the evidence, to delve a bit deeper to reveal the behaviour of the animal and above all to make you think like a detective.

Because they can be so elusive, mammals may be harder than birds to study, but then the results will be all the more rewarding and a great deal of fun can be had along the way.

As in the other Whittet Natural History Books, the text is liberally peppered with anecdotal accounts of personal observations and experiences, drawn from my wildlife travels and professional survey work. I count myself very fortunate to have been given the opportunity to work on mammal distribution surveys and to have been able to spend most of my time 'out in the field', so I have tried to relay my first-hand experiences rather than repeat published information found in other textbooks and field guides.

The analogy of the police detective has been used throughout since the methods of detection and process of elimination are the same whether you are solving a crime or solving a mammal mystery.

So for the budding Sherlock Holmes or Inspector Morse of the mammal world I have divided the book into two parts. The first outlines the methods, techniques and skills necessary for effective detection. The chapters here include fieldcraft, how to observe without being observed; how to read the signs, with hints on the best conditions for tracking and how to use your ears as well as your eyes; where to look, and what you may encounter in different habitats. There is also an essential guide to the techniques used and equipment for surveillance; how to analyse and identify the prey remains found in owl pellets; being prepared for the unexpected and some accounts of the unusual species that have survived out of captivity. A chapter on mammals and the law is important for all detectives.

The second part forms an identification field guide devoted to the various types of clue and a final chapter that brings them all together. The chapters of the guide include a series of user-friendly, easy-to-follow keys and comparative annotated drawings that have been drawn from life at their actual size where possible. These cover respectively the glimpsed animal, tracks, droppings, places of refuge, feeding remains and other field signs. (I wanted to include a scratch-and-sniff key, but Whittet thought that with the rich smells of fox, badger, otter and polecat nobody would want to touch the book with a barge pole let alone buy it!)

This book is primarily concerned with the mammal species found in Britain, but the mammal detective will always find mammals to track down no matter where in the world he or she may go. The techniques described here are equally applicable at home or abroad, it's just that the further afield you go the more homework you need to do to find out what species you may encounter.

In the far flung places of the world there may be considerable gaps in the knowledge about the local mammals to which the mammal detective could make a real contribution.

The art of camouflage.

On the beat

Some mammal species, such as red deer, foxes and hares, that have been hunted or persecuted by man, understandably show a natural wariness of your presence and quickly disappear when you are seen, heard or even scented on the air. To watch these wary animals you may need to take an SAS style of approach, dressed in full camouflage clothing including a black balaclava with eye-slits; you will need to keep low to the ground, crawling through the vegetation. As with birdwatching, always carry binoculars as these allow you to keep your distance and have superb light gathering powers in the twilight.

Find yourself a vantage point, perhaps on a hillside, but remember not to let your shape stand out against the skyline, as once happened to me. I was finishing a riverbank search for otter signs late one winter's afternoon and the light was fading fast. Having found some excellent fresh spraint (the tarry droppings of the otter) under a small tractor bridge, I returned to wait at the bridge a while with the faint hope of glimpsing an otter. Almost immediately as I looked upstream I could see a bow wave heading my way and sure enough an otter's head appeared midstream about 30 metres from the bridge.

Forgetting the golden rule about not making sudden movements, I quickly raised my binoculars, my shape breaking the skyline. The otter saw me and stopped swimming. However, luck was with me as the current continued to bring the now floating otter directly to where I stood on the bridge. For what appeared to be hours, but was only seconds, we stared at each other before the otter realized he was only about 5 metres from me and dived under and quickly out of view.

On another lucky occasion I was crossing a low footbridge that spanned a 2 metre drain in a wetland reserve, when I glimpsed another otter swimming towards me. Slowly and quietly I sat on my haunches to one side of the bridge where my outline would be concealed by a large bush. I was hoping that the otter would allow me a good view as it continued to swim on and under the footbridge without noticing me. I wasn't seen but I did not expect what happened next. The otter came to the bridge and stopped under it on the opposite bank to me. It then clambered out up the bank to spraint on the edge of the footbridge and started to cross the bridge towards me. From its size and head shape I could see it was a small female. She was at least halfway across before she suddenly became aware I was there. I still hadn't moved and was trying hard not even to blink. The otter stopped dead, sniffing the air, and after a few seconds she slowly back-tracked to the point where she clambered out, slipping back into the water but leaving a trail of little wet footprints glistening on the boards of the bridge. That was the last I'll

Otter spraint site on tree-root saddle of bankside tree.

see of her, I thought, but no, to my amazement she reappeared under my side of the footbridge and clambered out to sniff at my boots. Again I remained as still as possible but she was unsure about me and snorted, dropping back into the water to re-emerge in the reeds. This time the otter stood upright on her back legs to take another look at me; again unsure, she snorted twice before slipping gently into the water and swimming leisurely away. I was still spellbound for a minute or two before rising from my position to examine where she had sprainted. It was still steaming.

Sitting very still and quiet close to a badger sett at dusk is one of the best ways to observe these animals. Position yourself downwind so that your scent is not carried to the sett entrances and try to get an unobstructed view, as the light may have almost gone by the time they emerge. Even in the half light the striped face of the badger is easily recognized, but they are very cautious when they first emerge and any sudden movement will send them straight back underground and it could be a very long wait until they next come out. Even if you are providing a feast for the biggest mosquitoes you have ever seen, try to brush them away by making a slow steady movement of the hand rather than a sudden swat.

Nearly all the mammal detectives that I know have good stories to tell about their badger-watching experiences and a friend of mine recalls his first ever attempt after reading all the books and being shown the location of his local sett. Setting out on his own one evening after school, Bob positioned himself 'textbook fashion' in good view of the sett but unwittingly sat right on top of two outlying entrances. After about thirty minutes of sitting motionless, three tiny fox cubs emerged from under his feet and played around his legs, for what seemed like hours, each taking it in turn to pounce on the other's tail or chase after leaves. Afraid to move, Bob found his legs had now got cramp and fifteen minutes must have passed when a returning adult came right up behind him and let out a loud warning yelp that made him jump with shock and sent the cubs darting back underground, never to be seen again. Worried he had disturbed the area, Bob stayed on for another five minutes and was just about to leave when a badger came trundling along the path. In sheer disbelief he watched the animal come right up and sniff his shoes which were in a real state, encrusted with jam and flour from his part-time job in a bakery. With a big snort of disgust the badger continued on its nightly wanderings, leaving him trembling with excitement, punching his arm in the air and miming, 'Yeah, yeah, yeah'! He was hooked.

The mammal detective's guide to mammal watching

Some mammal species are best chanced upon rather than deliberately looked for. It would be difficult, say, to go for a walk with the intention of watching weasels despite the fact that they are relatively common and widespread. But, whatever the species, you can improve your chances of a longer sighting rather than a fleeting glimpse (or none at all) by remembering the following ten golden rules:

1 Dawn and dusk are the best times for watching most mammal species, so wearing dark clothing will help to conceal you from the animals. Avoid noisy clothes or any item that jangles or crackles, since noise will travel far at these times of day.

2 There is an inverse ratio as to the number of sightings and length of observation made with the size of party of observers. You will definitely see a lot more animals when you are on your own and can walk slowly and quietly. The quality of the sighting improves too.

3 When approaching cross-roads, bridges or bends in pathways, slow your pace down and keep close to the vegetation; for instance, take a bend on the inside so you are against cover. Take time to scan along the path or watercourse for mammal shapes. With care you should be able to see the animal before it sees you.

4 On sighting a mammal, try slowly to blend into the vegetation by hiding your own shape, squat down if necessary.

5 Do not make sudden movements.

6. The longer you remain unobserved, unheard or unscented the longer and more rewarding the observation you will make.
7. Remember to try and keep the wind in your face as most mammals have a sense of smell far superior to ours.
8. If you wish to get nearer for a photograph or simply just a better look, approach slowly, against cover, keeping low to the ground or circumnavigate the animal again using the available cover (large rocks or trees and bushes).
9. If the animal spots you (as it will sooner or later) keep still and try not to present a human shape. The animal may accept your presence and continue what it was doing or may even be curious about you and come to investigate.
10. With practice you may even be able to call the animal to you by squeaking on the back of the hand through wet lips. This works particularly well with inquisitive stoats, weasels and young foxes. For bats such as noctules inside a tree hole roost, squeaking a shrill call through wet lips may result in their agitated reply revealing which tree they are in. Your own behaviour of walking through a wood squeaking at trees may however draw some strange looks from anyone passing, but then mammal detection is an eccentric behaviour in the eyes of most people.

Inquisitive family of weasels attracted by squeaking through wet lips.

Less wary mammals

Not all species are wary of humans and some, like hedgehogs, can be easily followed just a few paces behind provided you can keep quiet. Remember, the snapping of a twig under your foot will sound like a gunshot to the hedgehog. Even then the animal may just 'freeze' or curl up for a few moments before resuming its wanderings and foraging.

Other species can be encouraged into the garden and can be viewed in comfort from a window, sitting in an armchair. There are now many households with gardens backing on to woodland that actively encourage squirrels, foxes, badgers and even deer by putting food out in the garden. How about creating a small mammal table near a window to observe mice, voles and shrews coming to a bait of seeds and mealworms? These small mammals of the nightshift can be a rewarding change from the birds of the daytime. Bird tables can be modified with ramps and access routes. But remember to keep the cats indoors or they will think you have created a local takeaway just for them.

Watching bats emerge from their roosts can be another rewarding experience, and if you are fortunate to have a roost at your house why not sit outside at dusk in a comfortable chair to count them flying out against the skyline? The mammal detective would be eager to find out where they go to forage for insects, what landscape features act as flight-lines, what numbers are involved and how this changes with the season. Finding out what time they return back to the roost can be a spectacular experience since the individuals of the colony may gather together outside the entrance swirling around in the sky chasing one another. This is one of my favourite sights of the summer night.

Informants

One avenue of enquiry to find a rare or unusual species is to ask people who by the nature of their work may come into contact with wild mammals, e.g. farmers, foresters, gamekeepers and nature reserve wardens.

You may like to design a questionnaire to target particular groups of people about certain mammals. For instance I was able to get a good response about the whereabouts of water voles and mink by mailing angling clubs. Bat groups have also gained good bat roost information from questionnaires in Wildlife Trust's newsletters as well as those sent to roofing and building firms.

For specific surveys and local projects requests for information can be put out on local radio stations or in local newspapers and magazines. But be careful not to take all the responses at face value, you may need to verify the stories by personal interview to check on your informant's competence. I once had a sighting of an otter reported to me that on investigation turned out to be a water vole! On another occasion an excellent 'textbook' description of a pine marten was backed up by a photograph of the same animal that was obviously a stoat with its short thin black-tipped tail. People sometimes see what they want to see!

The art of reading the signs

The mammal detective should not only be able to identify which mammal footprints, droppings or feeding remains have been found but also interpret some of the behaviour revealed by the signs. For example, droppings may be a territory marker; footprints may tell whether the animal was walking or travelling at speed; its direction of travel; whether it was hunting or commuting; the number of animals involved; any social interactions; if hunting, whether it was successful or not, and what was eaten.

Under the right conditions and circumstances all this information can be interpreted from the field evidence. Thus by reading the signs it is possible to understand what has taken place hours before, usually under the cover of darkness, without actually needing to see the animal in question.

Tracking in the snow

Best tracking conditions undoubtedly occur when there is a blanket of lying snow, which can reveal the passage of most mammal species that are active during the winter months (except certain small mammal species that are active beneath the snow covering – their tunnelling and foraging activity only becomes apparent after the snow melts, revealing a network of criss-crossed runs on the surface. Piles of soil show entrances to deeper burrows and well frequented latrines are easily spotted.)

Lying snow can often be the only way to reveal the presence of our rarer and more elusive mammals such as the pine marten or wildcat. If the blanket is extensive then the tracks may allow the animal to be followed over a large distance, showing where it hunted (if a predator) and the tracks of its quarry. Following the tracks may also reveal the animal's lair or lying-up place, even where the animal is actually hiding away at that moment.

On one memorable occasion I was able to follow the tracks of a pine marten for a distance of over three miles, finding where it crossed a stream from boulder to boulder, its bounding gait often shown by the hind feet overprinting the fore feet. Snow had been dug up where the marten had heard a vole in its run below. It travelled completely on the ground, except at one place where it had climbed an old rowan tree for a few of the shrivelled berries that remained; it had left its scat (dropping) on a prominent rock (showing vole fur and bones with a few rowanberry seeds) and investigated a series of rock piles in a zigzagging path. It crossed open ground at speed (indicated by the spacing of the footprints) and took a more leisurely pace while following a forest track through a young spruce plantation. Here more scats were left on top of older ones and its own tracks were crossed by another marten. The trail eventually petered out at the foot of a small crag where there was a jumble of boulder scree providing a thousand potential den sites.

Tracks in snow can often reveal events that took place hours beforehand.

On the slopes of a snow-covered Scottish mountain, I spent another day following tracks of various mammals, red deer, fox, pine marten and mountain hare. The hare tracks were particularly abundant but the animal's white winter coat proved very effective camouflage amongst the scattered rocks. I followed one set of tracks to within 4 metres of the sitting hare and still failed to see it until it suddenly shot away with a great burst of speed. On the slope nearby I found the distinctive trail of a fox lying directly over that of a mountain hare that it was obviously hunting. The two trails twisted and turned, both animals kicking up a flurry of snow as the hare changed direction in the chase. It soon became apparent that the fox on this occasion was no match for its quarry as the footprints revealed that it had lost ground as the hare outran its pursuer; after what was probably over 1,500 metres the out-manoeuvred fox finally gave up to look for some easier prey or perhaps some carrion.

Following the trail of a brown hare across a flat arable field in winter I noticed that the animal had a cunning method of trying to throw any hunting fox or dog off its scent. At frequent intervals the animal back-tracked over its own tracks for a metre or so and then made a big jump to the side before continuing in a different direction with a great spurt of speed. The tracks left by a field full of 'mad March hares' are even more confusing!

Snow-covered river banks may reveal one field sign that is widely known but rarely encountered — the otter slide, where the animal toboggans on its belly, ploughing a smooth channel down the snow slope. One can imagine the animal enjoying the experience so much that it will climb back up the slope to do it again, although I personally have never found signs that they actually do this.

Tracking on sand and mud

You don't have to wait for the first fall of snow in order to go mammal tracking: a trip to the sand dune areas of Britain's coast at any time of year will reveal an expanse of footprint-laden sand. Water-margins always present a soft substrate (i.e. silt and mud) that will register footprints. In fact when river courses have dropped to their summer low some excellent conditions for finding tracks occur.

Watercourses may act as highways along which mammals travel, places for foraging and drinking or simply natural boundaries to the animal's home-range.

Some species, such as the water vole, may live their entire lives beside the water margin, foraging on the luxuriant vegetation and burrowing in the bank. This readily allows the mammal detective to find its tracks, latrines, feeding remains and burrows.

I spent two happy years travelling the length and breadth of mainland Britain carrying out the first systematic survey of the distribution of water voles. Selecting sites from Ordnance Survey maps in designated 10 kilometre squares, I visited a total of 2,970 localities. At each site I searched the water margin for water vole signs for a distance of 600 metres. This way each site could be recorded on a standardized survey form, noting the same information on habitat and the frequency of sign, if present. Mink evidence (tracks and droppings) were also recorded. So, without having to observe the animals directly, a comprehensive picture was gained as to the distribution ranges and the relative abundance of both species in different parts of the country. The water vole's preferred habitat requirements were determined and a relationship between the local abundance of mink (predator) and the relative abundance of water voles (prey item) was suggested.

Tracking in grasslands and woodlands

Away from water and under drier conditions the art of reading the signs requires a bit more practice, as footprints may not register. Here mammal trails still occur as trampled vegetation, sometimes as obvious 'runs' worn bare by frequent use, although more often than not just registering as a temporary pushing aside of the leaves. At dawn such short-lived trails can be very obvious among the dew-laden vegetation and by following these, damp ground may show an imprint of which

The distinctive otter slide.

mammal was involved. Trails running into field boundaries such as hedges or wire fences may converge on a regular crossing point and again an imprint could be searched for or even a tuft of hair caught on a thorny branch, bramble bush or barbed wire. Where the animal has passed through a hedge the 'tunnel' size in the vegetation may give a further clue to its identity. A rabbit obviously makes a much smaller tunnel than a fox or muntjac deer.

In woodland, mammal trails tend to criss-cross throughout, but some form distinct thoroughfares, being used by many different species. Where there are no tracks, remember to look for other signs, droppings being the most obvious.

At certain times of the year there is heightened activity and more signs to be encountered. During the rutting season roe bucks will fray the bark of young saplings with their antlers and scratch bare patches of soil with their cleaves (divided hooves). Another curious sign left by the rutting roe is that of a well worn path in a tight circle or figure of eight around a tree stump caused by the animal repeatedly running the same route, perhaps in pursuit of a doe in heat. This is known as a 'roe ring'.

Beside badger setts and fox earths, flattened vegetation and strewn debris show where the cubs have been at play. Fox cubs in particular can devastate an area around the den trampling and digging up plants, chewing wood, bone and bits of plastic, leaving food remains scattered all over the place and turning the whole area into a bare arena for their rough-and-tumble games. Old bedding will also be seen near the entrances.

At the other end of the spectrum small mammals such as harvest mice or shrews can scurry about all over the place and barely leave any evidence that they have been there. Mice and voles reveal their presence by caches of food (usually seeds) and chopped vegetation taken to a favoured eating place that is usually hidden from the view of avian predators. By searching through the short grasses and herbaceous plants, the low vole tunnels can be quickly found, especially where the vegetation is matted. On calm days one can stand still and quiet, taking an aerial view over a piece of rough grassland, in much the same way as a kestrel would hunt; the tell-tale activity of voles, mice and shrews may be observed as movement of individual grass blades, quivering flower stalks or sometimes the tugging of succulent leaves. Listen for the scurrying sounds from the leaf litter or the shrill cries of territorial disputes and social contact calls, especially among the shrews.

Squirrels and dormice spend most of their time in tree branches but show their presence by discarding feeding remains from above and so these tend to be where the food source occurs.

How to use your ears

When walking through a woodland, it often pays to stop, close your eyes and listen for the sounds and calls of mammals. A squirrel may soon be discovered by listening for the sound of falling debris such as bits of pine cone. Squirrel disputes

Mobbing bird alarm calls tell of a predator's whereabouts.

and chases can be very noisy affairs with the animals so engrossed in chattering and crashing through the treetop branches that the mammal detective can sneak right up close to watch. At night sound seems to be magnified and will carry for a long way, even the rustling of a woodmouse among the leaves sounds like an animal the size of a wild boar! The night is also the time some species make territorial calls, the eerie screaming yelp of a fox may sound like someone being murdered. Roe deer and muntjac may bark an alarm call while the red deer in rut cries a deep throaty roar. Most species are silent for most of the time but mating behaviour always tends to be accompanied by some noise: even the hedgehog will make very loud snorting and huffing sounds. Family groups also noisily give their presence away as youngsters jostle with one another for food or in play.

Using the mobbing behaviour of birds and other mammals can also help find elusive predators. Hunters of the night often lie up during the day in dense cover or may even sit out 'sunbathing' when the weather permits. In such locations their inactivity may allow them to go unobserved by people but not their potential prey – birds of all kinds quickly gather round the the predator and chatter, scold and generally mob it, creating a lot of noise attracting attention until the animal moves away into deeper cover or further afield.

Even a predator out travelling, hunting or stalking is at risk from discovery by vigilant eyes and then up goes the alarm cry, calls pointing to its presence and even telling which predator it is. In India, trained tiger trackers use the 'calls from the jungle' to interpret the whereabouts of a tiger – honks from peacocks, barks from sambhar, chital and muntjac deer and cries from langur monkeys (the langur emitting a different cry again for the leopard, its main predator).

African baboons are among those with the widest range of alarm calls: they warn of lion, leopard, cheetah, hyena, crocodile, python, venomous snakes or various species of eagle or hawk.

In Britain, I have found that blackbirds, thrushes, magpies, robins and wrens will readily scold foxes and members of the weasel family (mustelids), as well as owls, hawks and falcons. So it's always worth investigating the commotion caused by these birds.

Hares standing upright could be watching the passage of a fox, judging its distance and calculating when to run away should it come too close.

Otters are often mobbed by gulls, perhaps for scraps of fish but more readily during the nesting season when the otter may take the occasional egg or chick.

Gulls, terns, shearwaters and gannets may follow a school of dolphins or pod of whales to their feeding grounds, taking advantage of the shoals of fish driven to the surface.

Patient sitting, watching and waiting are all necessary skills practised by the complete mammal detective: do not be put off by your disappointments, keep trying, you'll find the successes will seem all the sweeter.

Right time, right place

Some species of mammal, such as the bats, are completely nocturnal but most are active at dawn and dusk, hiding themselves away during the daylight hours. Although you may find signs of them during the day, sightings will only be divulged to those who get up early or go to bed late.

In addition to a day-night activity rhythm, mammals also show seasonal changes in activity of which the mammal detective should be aware. In spring and summer most species show signs of breeding activity, perhaps occupying a defended territory, and are preoccupied with rearing young. Tracks of the young animals can often be seen closely following those of the adult and the playful but inexperienced youngster is more likely to be seen, especially in the long drawn-out evenings. In the autumn there seems to be an abundance of mammal activity with most populations being at their largest and young animals beginning to disperse. Before the first frosts many species feed furiously to build up fat for hibernation or put down caches of stored food for later in the winter. Other species may mate in the autumn so that the young can be born in the spring. This would be the best time to go looking for rutting red deer, mating roosts of bats or hunting for hazelnuts distinctively opened by dormice.

The period of winter is a time of hibernation for bats, dormice, hedgehogs and to a lesser extent badgers and squirrels. Carnivores may be forced to hunt more out in the open, as cover is reduced and small mammals may spend longer periods underground so encounters will be limited to fewer species, but a covering of snow will make the tracks easier to find. This is perhaps the best season for the beginner to start – by looking for the clear tracks and traces left by the reduced number of species.

Where to look

The British countryside provides a wide variety of habitat types, from the harsh environment of the windswept high mountain tops to the sheltered environment of the ancient deciduous coppiced woodland; from mountain rivers and rugged sea lochs to meandering lowland watercourses and shallow ponds. Some natural habitats are rapidly disappearing, such as lowland heaths and water meadows, while others have been created, such as extensive conifer plantations, roadside verge grasslands and suburban gardens.

All provide a home to mammals and the diligent detective will find clues to the various species that live in each habitat. The task of detective work is made a little easier since not all species occur in every habitat and some may even be restricted to one preferred habitat in one geographical area.

Discussed below are the different habitat types and the typical assemblage of

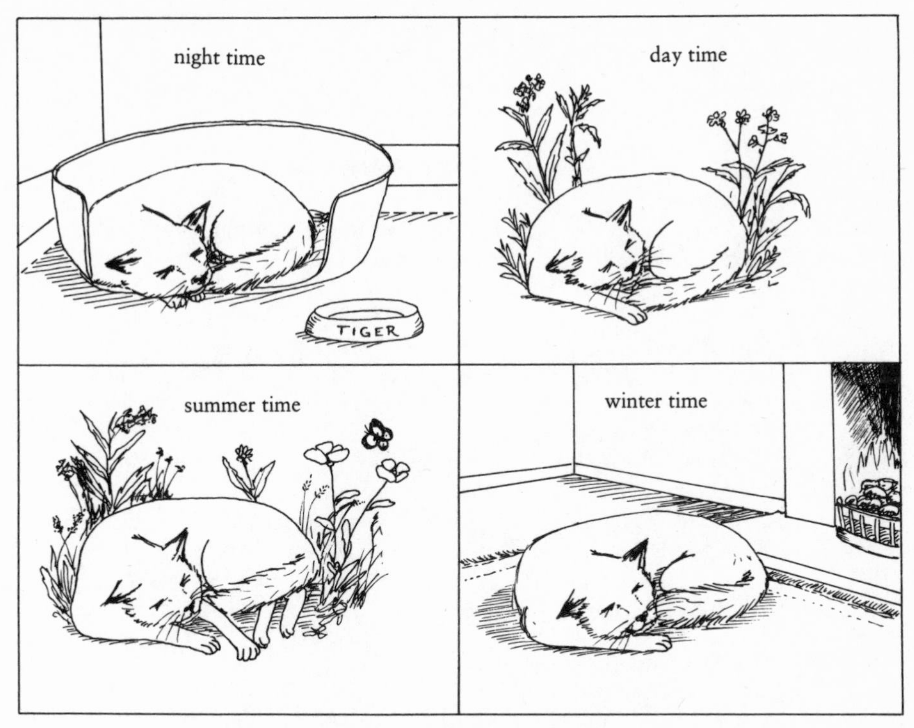

The activity pattern of a domestic cat.

mammal species that they support. It should be remembered, however, that mammals are mobile and often move between habitats and that the habitats themselves are not always easily defined, one merging into another.

Britain was once a very wooded island and many of our native mammals, both large and small, still make their homes in the trees. A canopy of trees and shrubs provides mammals with shelter from both wind and cold weather. Holes and hollows in trees or among tree roots also provide a secure place of refuge. In addition, for those species that can climb, the branches provide space in which to live and forage for food. **Deciduous woodlands** contain a wide variety of tree, shrub and flower species, all available in different seasons. This provides mammals with a year-round opportunity to forage on leaves, buds, flowers, seeds, fruits and bark, not to mention the vast number of invertebrates and fungi that may be eaten. It has been calculated that a single coppiced woodland of around 65 hectares (161 acres) can support 5,000 mice and voles, together with shrews, moles, squirrels and bats, as well as, possibly, dormice, weasels, badgers, foxes and deer.

Coniferous forests will also provide a diversity of mammal species, but the species composition varies, depending on the age and structure of the woodland.

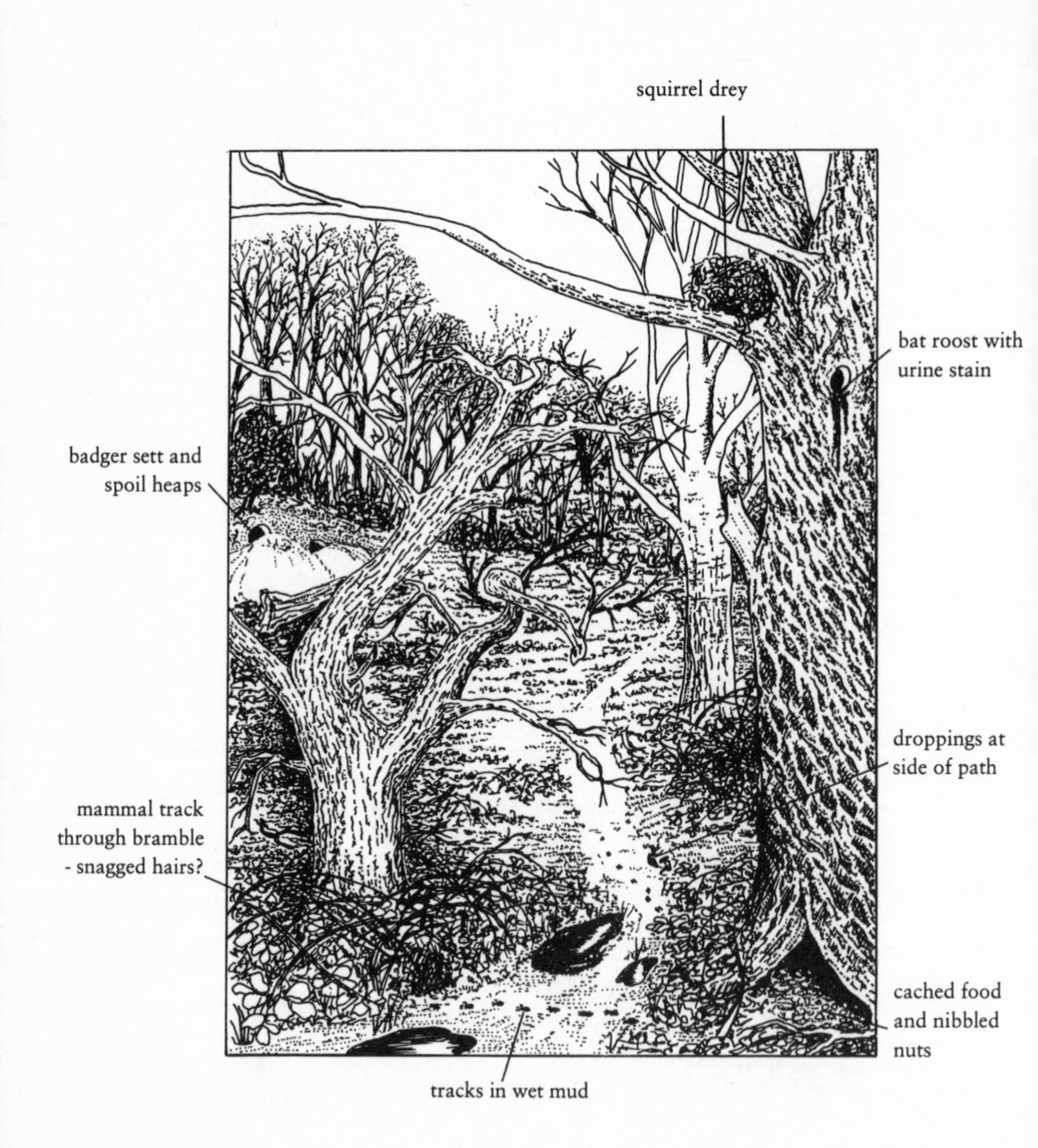

WHERE TO LOOK IN WOODLANDS

Very young plantations and clear felled areas can support a high density of small mammals among the coarse grasses, particularly the field vole. However, as soon as the canopy becomes closed and dense, very little light reaches the ground, which becomes bare and the small mammal population virtually disappears. Cone-bearing trees provide squirrels with a year-round source of food and the plantations of northern Britain are among the last strongholds for the red squirrel. These woodlands also support large populations of roe deer which may cause damage to the young trees by fraying bark when they clean their antlers and by browsing accessible shoots. Among the open areas of the Scottish glens and mountains, the conifer plantations shelter foxes, pine martens, wildcats, badgers and deer.

Watercourses of all kinds and their associated marshland and fringing habitats are attractive to many mammals, offering food and shelter as well as drinking water. Riparian plants are often tall and luxuriant, providing on the doorstep food and cover for water voles and other small mammals. The tall reeds close to the water's edge also provide a nest site for the harvest mouse. The damp waterside soils are full of invertebrates, especially worms and insect larvae, on which shrews, moles and badgers feed; the water itself supports a vast diversity of aquatic invertebrate larvae, which emerge in their thousands as they become adult — great food for bats. Tree-lined banks provide places of refuge for bats when suitable tree holes occur and cavities among the tree roots may give shelter to otters and mink.

The soft water margin can show up mammal footprints, especially the tracks of the smaller rodents and shrews on the fine silt. As well as the animals that live in an aquatic environment, look for the tracks of mammals that come to drink at the water's edge, such as badgers, foxes and deer.

Grasslands, downlands, pasture and other open areas such as arable farmland are home to a number of mammal species, but few are likely to be seen during the day, the animals preferring to stay hidden in cover or underground and only venturing out at night. The mammal detective will soon find the tell-tale clues to the presence of rabbits and hares, moles, hedgehogs, mice, voles and shrews as well as weasels, stoats, badgers, foxes and deer. However, the detective needs to take care not to confuse the footprints, droppings and hair tufts (caught on strands of barbed wire or thorn bushes) of wild mammals with those of domestic farm animals, since the grasslands may be used for grazing by sheep, cattle and horses (some fields may even support free-range pigs!).

Rough pasture of tall grasses, rushes, sedges, thistles and nettlebeds on uneven ground can support very high densities of small mammals (densities of 500 per hectare are not uncommon for the field vole in a good 'vole' year).

Hedgerows and field boundaries may act as corridors for mammals by linking up blocks of woodland. It is thought that a good dense hedgerow is important for the dispersal of polecats and that, without these links between woodland blocks, isolated populations of species such as dormice or red squirrels are vulnerable to extinction. Boundary hedges and tree lines are also linear features that provide bats with a flyway on which they can commute from roost site to feeding areas.

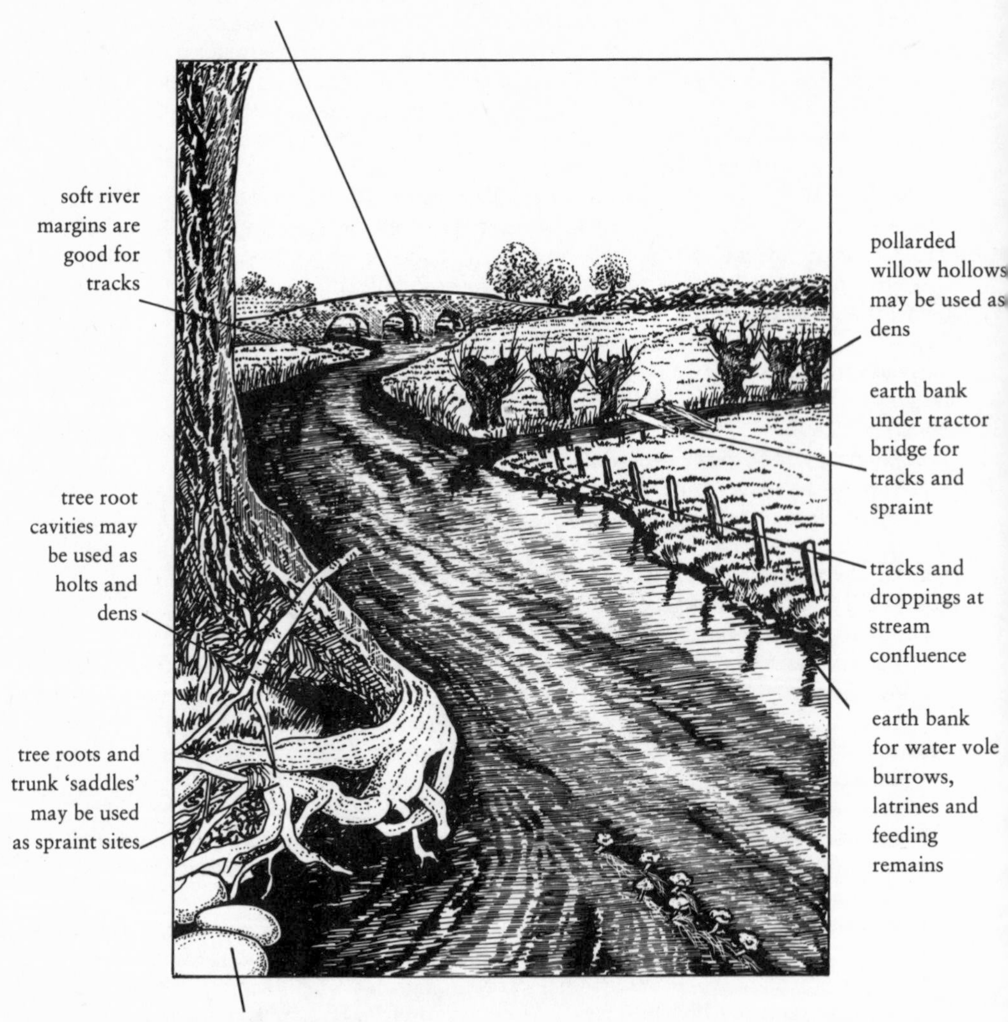

WHERE TO LOOK ALONG WATERCOURSES

Coastal clifftops give a good vantage point from which to 'sea watch' for the passage of whales, dolphins and seals but also be on the lookout for otters and mink, particularly around Britain's rocky shoreline and estuaries. The most productive sea watching is best done in the company of others; then you can split the area being watched into sections (imagine you are looking at the hours of a clock face, straight ahead being 12 o'clock, to the right 12–3, and to the left 9–12).

Features such as ships on the horizon and peculiar tide currents also help to pinpoint positions, e.g. 'breaching minke whale between that tanker on the horizon and us, heading left at about 11 o'clock'! It may only be in view for a few seconds so you will need to be able to home in on it quickly. At peak passage times you never know what may turn up (see pp. 60-63 for what might be seen).

By searching the strandline you may also be able to find corpses or bits of bone washed up from sea mammals that have died out at sea.

At the other extreme are Britain's **mountains**, but most are not very high; only in two Scottish regions (Grampian and Highland) does the terrain surpass a height of 1,200 metres (4,000 feet). Nevertheless, they are bleak places for mammals to live, especially in winter when they are snow-covered and chilled by strong winds. These upland sites may be home to herds of red deer and in a few places feral goats. Other mammals may include the mountain hare and stoat; the coats of both of these change to white in winter for camouflage against the snow. Pine marten, fox and wildcat may range over these high slopes when out hunting, whilst among the small mammals the field vole and pygmy shrew are the most abundant. On wetter ground both mole and water vole may be found. (The 1989-90 water vole survey located the presence of these animals to an altitude of 660 metres/2,100 feet in Scotland.)

Although trees rarely grow on these windswept uplands, shelter is provided among the thickets of bilberry and heather or among rocks. Where you see meadow pipits and wheatears at such sites you can be sure there are plenty of small insects about, making it a good place to look for the pygmy shrew.

In winter the larger mammals move to lower ground, although you may still find their footprints on the snow-covered slopes. The small mammals, however, do not make the migration down the slopes but survive under the blanket of snow, hidden from view until the snow melts, revealing their workings among the flattened vegetation.

Lowland heaths support a similar community of mammals to the upland moors but, due to their restricted distribution, mountain hares, pine martens and wildcats are absent. Instead, rabbits may feature more abundantly and roe deer are the commonest of the deer species to be encountered. Which mammals are to be found largely depends on the structure of the heath and its adjacent habitats. The more wooded a locality the greater the likelihood of deer and the richer the community of small mammals. The presence of ponds or a waterway will make the occurrence of bats more likely.

Man is continually creating a new habitat in the form of the urban/suburban

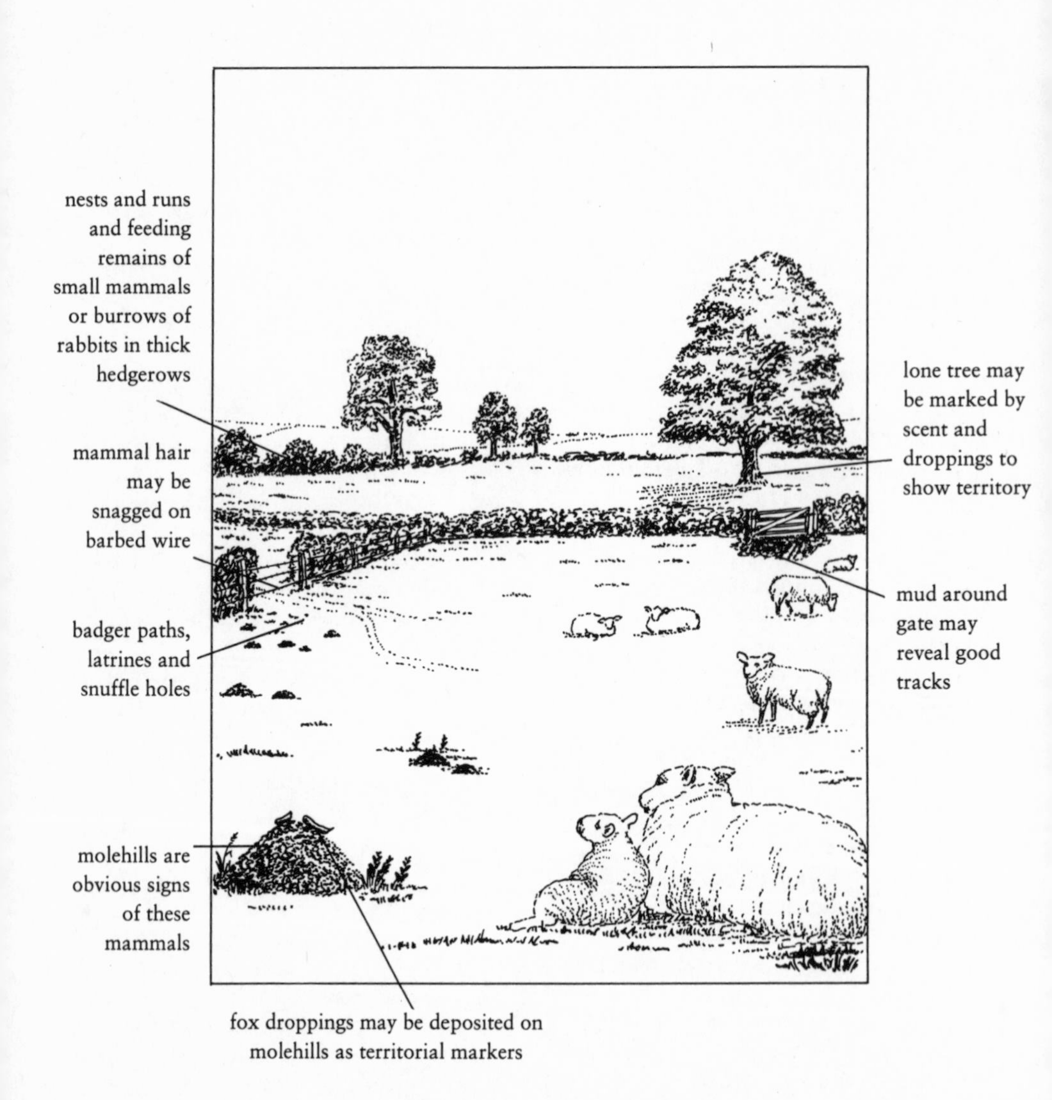

WHERE TO LOOK IN PASTURE

environment linked by an extensive network of roads and railways. Some mammal species have been quick to adapt to this changing world, living alongside man in his buildings and gardens. Most notable of these species are the bats, house mouse, brown rat, hedgehog, fox and, where there are sufficient trees, the grey squirrel.

As with roads, railway lines bisect many different habitats but, because they provide less disturbance, there are opportunities for mammal encounters. Watching the track from a safe vantage point such as a bridge or even from a train itself you may spot the animals that utilize the track, embankments or nearby fields such as foxes, badgers, rabbits, hares, voles and deer. Disused railway lines are often converted into footpaths and so are a good place to start looking for the mammals that use these corridors linking other habitats.

The broad verges of **motorways** and trunk roads offer a relatively undisturbed corridor of grassland and scrub. Here rabbits, moles, voles, mice and shrews thrive despite traffic noise and vibration. However, crossing the roads can be a problem for all mammals especially at night and thousands fall victim to road traffic accidents every year. Discarded bottles and drink cans at roadside lay-bys may present a further problem to small mammals, since they will often go inside to explore or look for food and fail to get out again. The mammal detective may find the remains of mice, voles and shrews by the dozen in such thoughtlessly discarded deathtraps (see the Forensics chapter to help you identify these remains). Other pieces of rubbish, especially large items of metal, wood, plastic or cardboard, may provide shelter and a suitable nest site for small mammals. By carefully lifting such items the runs and nests may be seen. Other animals such as foxes may scavenge for food scraps around litter bins and their droppings may often show pieces of plastic (I once found a pine marten dropping at a Scottish picnic site that consisted entirely of a clear plastic bag, all twisted and moulded into the typical dropping shape and smelling strongly of 'eau d'marten' – I don't think the animal could have satisfied its hunger that day).

Lifted corrugated iron sheet reveals field vole runs, nest and latrine.

The flat-mammal detective!

As we hurry about in our cars it soon becomes obvious that many species are tragically killed on the roads every day. Even more so at night as the animal, dazzled by the headlights, 'freezes' in the path of oncoming vehicles or tries to dash across in front of the cars coming from both directions.

For the mammal detective this provides an opportunity to census the local elusive mammal population and even confirm the presence of a rare species by way of an unfortunate corpse. In the late summer of 1993 a road-killed otter, a mere 12 miles from outer London, provided the first 'hard evidence' that the species had finally returned to the River Thames catchment after being absent for twenty years.

The spread of the polecat back into the English Midlands from its Welsh stronghold is being successfully monitored and mapped by recording the distribution of road kills. These dead animals are also being collected for detailed examination by experts to determine how genetically pure the individuals are. That is, measurements of the body and skulls, together with DNA material for genetic fingerprinting, are used to look at the incidence of hybridization with escaped ferrets.

Of course it's not just the rarities that provide material for study. Since 1990 Dr Pat Morris of the Mammal Society has been carrying out a hedgehog road kill survey, using volunteers to record the frequency of flattened individuals seen on each car journey over twenty miles in distance.

Hedgehog road kills survey 1990-92

The hedgehog is one of the most popular British mammals; it is common and has a widespread distribution and is easy to recognize even when flattened on a road surface! However, there have been few studies of population size or regional variation in their numbers. This survey attempts to provide data on trends in the various hedgehog populations.

Volunteers completed record sheets for each journey driven in July, August and September (the same journey not repeated in the same month), noting the mileage and location at the beginning and end of each journey. It was important to standardize the results so all recording should have commenced before the first dead hedgehog was seen and it was equally important to record any journeys when no specimens were encountered. Any hedgehogs seen dead on the road were recorded, together with the

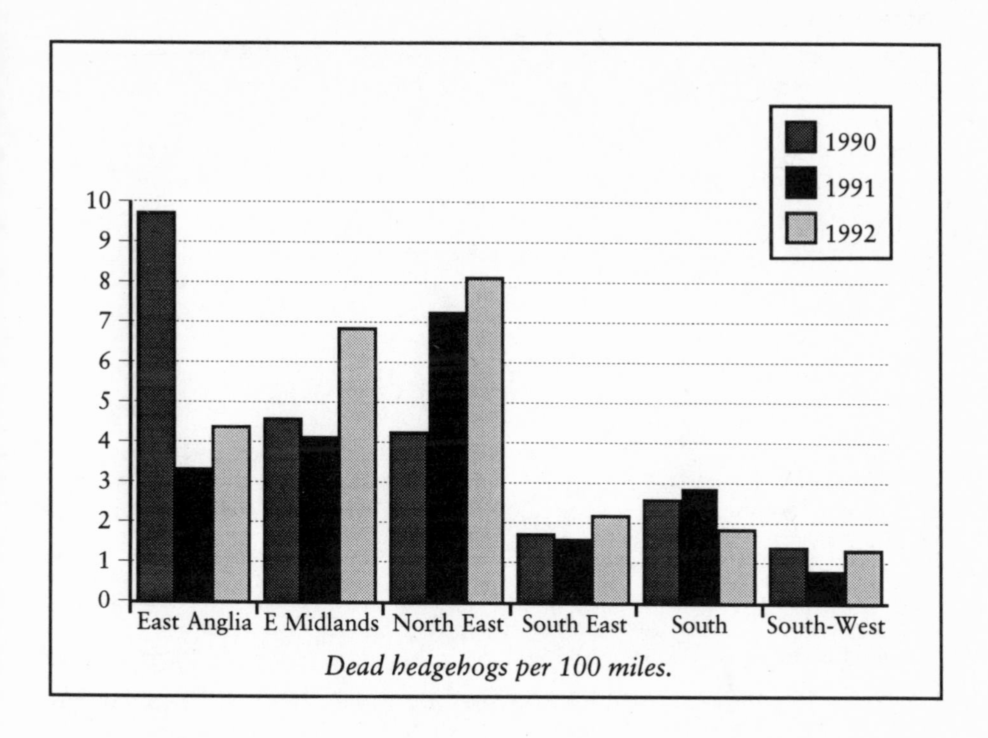

Dead hedgehogs per 100 miles.

milometer reading, the nearest town, county and habitat type either side of the road (by ticking the relevent boxes on the form). Recorders were asked not to count in towns more than 5 miles across, on motorways, at night or in the rain. In total 35,720 miles of road were surveyed in 1990 and 1,187 dead hedgehogs counted. In 1991, 37,977 miles of road revealed 1,305 flat hedgehogs and in 1992, 832 dead hedgehogs were counted in 28,996 miles of non-motorway road driven.

The submitted record sheets were then sorted into the appropriate regions of England, Scotland and Wales and the number of hedgehogs per mile calculated for each journey. These data were then converted to numbers per 100 miles driven for each region (see graph above).

As you can see there was a wide variation between regions and this was remarkably similar for each of the three years. The North East, East Midlands and East Anglia consistently show the highest numbers of hedgehogs per 100 miles whereas the South-West was ranked bottom in all three years. This suggests a real geographical difference in population size and not just differences in traffic density.

In addition to information on the

relative abundance of the hedgehog, the flat-mammal detectives were able to show that many of the road kills were clumped together suggesting that these animals often use the same places to cross the road and this may be related to habitat features.

Contrary to what you might expect, one third of the hedgehogs came from arable areas, another third from grassland but only a sixth of the records were from urban areas (even fewer from roads that passed through woodlands).

Many of the casualties of the night are cleared away by an army of scavengers on the lookout for an easy meal. Foxes, crows and gulls probably remove most of the smaller corpses in the early hours of daylight. Censuses for these species would probably underestimate their frequency.

Trying to identify squashed animals from a moving car without stopping is a difficult skill to master, but a number of commoner species are soon recognized. In fact, it is possible to categorize mammals into those most likely to be encountered flat on the road.

1 The most likely species are animals that are very common, widespread and are fairly large and easy to spot. This group includes the following (given in descending order of frequency): rabbit, hedgehog, fox, hare and badger.

2 This group includes those animals that are widespread but less commonly killed. These are also fairly large and easy to spot: grey squirrel, mink, stoat, domestic cat, brown rat, weasel.

3 This group includes the rarely encountered large and medium sized mammals: deer species, otter, pine marten, polecat, red squirrel and mountain hare.

4 This final group includes those animals that because of their small size are very difficult to spot flattened on the road and are almost impossible to distinguish without careful in the hand examination: dormice, mole, mice, voles, shrews and bats

Remember, if you do try to spot and identify mammal road kills while in a vehicle as the driver or passenger, take care and pay due attention to the road and other traffic. If there is something dead on the road that looks unusual and interesting requiring further investigation, pull off the road safely and walk back. Do not cause obstruction to other road users. (It is an offence to stop on a motorway except in an emergency and it would be extremely dangerous and foolish to try and retrieve a corpse from such a road.)

Countryside lanes and roads can be safely walked or cycled along and this slower pace of travel will allow you to find more of the smaller mammals killed by traffic. I once found a fresh dead Natterer's bat in perfect condition next to a very flat and barely identifiable pipistrelle (examination revealed the distinctive post calcarial lobe by its foot, see illustration on p. 75 bat parade), obviously a black spot for bats where the road crossed a mature hedge and treeline.

The network of roads in Britain, as in many other countries, carves up the landscape, cutting through the hidden routes that the wild animals have traditionally used for centuries, putting them at risk from road traffic accidents. The integrity of these wildlife corridors, be they woodlands, hedges or watercourses, is being continually eroded and fragmented. The problem is likely to become worse as we move to an increasingly car-dependent society, building faster, straighter new roads to carry an increasing density of traffic day and night.

The mammal detective can use the tracks and trails of mammals to help identify potential black spots at the planning stages of road building. Wildlife reflectors, suitable fencing and specially designed underpasses are some solutions that can be cheaply put in place during construction. On existing roads where animals are already being regularly killed, evidence collected by the mammal detective can be used to make a case for the installation of similar solutions (although to dig up a road to put in an underpass is usually prohibitively expensive). Warning road signs and speed restrictions at black spots could also be used.

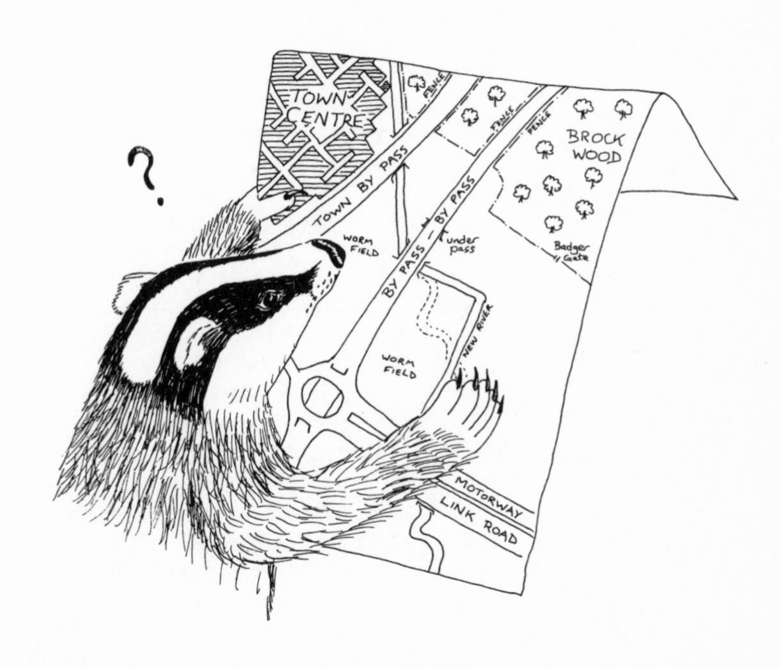

Surveillance and the collection of evidence

Even if you just intend to go out and look for mammals for your own personal pleasure, it pays to be methodical and keep a record of your observations. This chapter describes how you can collect evidence and what equipment you may need.

The written evidence: why you need it and how to use it

A field notebook is essential to record your observations directly as they happen. *Write it down now.* You will soon forget all the important details if you don't and accurate dated records are essential data for distribution maps and the long-term monitoring of a species' status in both local and national recording schemes. Your notes needn't be as detailed as 'I was proceeding in a northerly direction when ...' but should include date, species, location (six-figure grid reference if possible); what was seen and any comments. Your observations may seem trivial at the time but they may build up to form a more interesting story. For instance a fleeting glimpse of what you believe was a rarity may not stand on its own but if several people also observed the same species in the same locality within the same period of time then more weight is given to your single glimpse.

Find out where your local Biological Records Centre is (usually a County Museum) and see if they are carrying out any particular surveys. All records submitted to them help revise distribution maps at both local and national level. Regular reviews of distribution data and surveys of status all help to monitor population trends in species. Without the monitoring, we may not realize that a species is declining until it is too late to put in place an active conservation measure that may reverse the trend. Some species, such as water voles, harvest mice and the shrews, may be disappearing from your local patch without anyone noticing (until they become conspicuous by their total absence). Other species may be making a recovery following a population decline and contracted distribution; you may be able to show that the species is becoming more populous and expanding its range, by finding field signs where they have not been found before.

The National Otter Surveys have shown just that by surveying the same series of mapped and referenced sites at seven-year intervals. In England alone, 3,188 sites were searched for otter signs and the most recent findings (1991-94 survey) have demonstrated a most encouraging and dramatic spread along many river systems. Other species may also be spreading through Britain and these need to be monitored because they are non-native, e.g. introduced/escaped exotics such as the American mink, grey squirrel, edible dormouse, sika deer, muntjac and Chinese water deer.

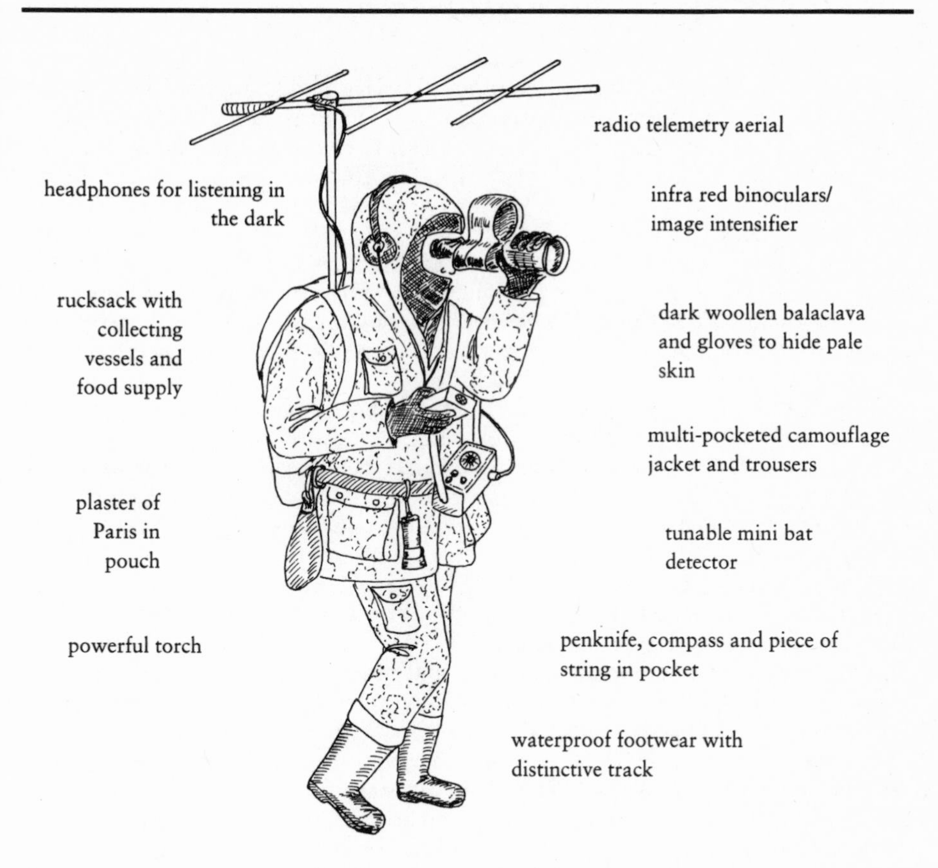

The ultimate mammal detective.

Essential equipment

You might imagine that the modern mammal detective needs to be loaded down with all the latest technology and bleeping gadgets but actually your best equipment comes free! That is, sharp vision, acute hearing and a keen sense of smell. The ability to put yourself in the right place at the right time also helps but this is often a combination of luck and experience. Further essentials have to be bought, borrowed or received as birthday or Christmas presents.

The first of these is a good pair of binoculars. Apart from letting you watch mammals, binoculars allow you to examine mud banks for footprints from a bridge or the opposite bank of a river, they let you spot otter spraint on midstream boulders when you would otherwise need a complete wetsuit to wade through the torrent or they can transport you into the tall branches of a tree to check out a squirrel drey. Times ten magnification would be the best, with 10 x 40s or 10 x 50s giving the best field of view and excellent light-gathering capacity, especially in the twilight of dusk or dawn. Even on very dark nights it's amazing just how much more can be observed using binoculars. Of course, a night-viewing scope that either works by image intensifying or infra-red (body heat) detection is an even better piece of equipment for nocturnal work. Fantastic technology for the more serious mammal detective, allowing the animals to be watched undisturbed in near total darkness.

Telescopes and spotting scopes have their uses but in my opinion are not as versatile as a trusty 'pair of bins', tending to be a bit cumbersome and normally requiring the use of a tripod. However, if you are already going to be carrying a 'scope around for your birdwatching interest then it will certainly help you pick out and identify mammals at a distance.

The next useful piece of equipment is a torch, not so much for shining at mammals during the hours of darkness, although it's a rewarding experience to watch bats passing through a hand-held beam of light when they fly and feed over water. The mammal detective also carries his torch during the day for shining into dark places such as recesses under bridges, or among riverbank tree roots for signs of some of our more elusive species. It's also useful for peering into tree hollows which a mammal may be using as a place of refuge. I once got the shock of my life when I crawled into the base of an old hollowed-out pollarded willow looking for otter spraint and mink scats (as you do!). There was a strong musky odour but I was not expecting to come up against a wall of coarse hair as I bumped into a sleeping badger. I've never moved so quickly in my life as I shot out backwards. The badger just carried on snoring!

Collecting vessels and sealable polythene bags are another must to take out into the field by the truckload. Plastic film canisters are excellent for small fragile items you wish to take home for later examination. These could be bat droppings or fresh otter spraint (my car is full of them). Sealable 'freezer' bags, especially those that allow you to write on them (date, location, grid reference, etc.), are excellent for collecting droppings for later diet analysis, owl pellets for later dissection or samples of feeding remains such as chewed pine cones or gouged-out hazelnut shells. All sorts of material can help build up a useful reference collection (although some of the smellier items have a very short shelf life and are usually sent back where they came from or assigned to a deep hole and buried in the back garden). A freezer is a brilliant piece of equipment for the mammal detective. It also helps to live in a tolerant household (or one that has lost its sense of smell).

You can make use of almost any dead specimen you encounter and build up your own collection of mammal skins, perhaps small mammals killed by a cat or examples of fine pelts from road casualties. Dead shrews, mice and voles may be skinned, treated with borax or alum salt and stretched over a finger of stiff card (known as 'carded small mammals') and then labelled for reference. Hair samples from these can be compared in any forensic work (see next chapter). Intact skulls and bones can also be retrieved from corpses and cleaned up by boiling in an old saucepan like some bizarre witch's broth! For really white skulls a weak solution of bleach followed by sun drying really does the trick.

Again for building a reference collection or as a permanent keepsake of particularly good examples, the mammal detective carries material for making plastercasts of mammal imprints. This usually means a small bag of plaster of Paris, a vessel for collecting or containing water and strips of card to be fastened with a paperclip forming a versatile way of containing the mixed plaster that's poured over the footprint.

How to make the perfect plastercast

Making a collection of plastercasts is the best way to study mammal tracks in three dimensions and no drawing or photograph can reproduce the fine detail quite so well. The technique is very simple. Water and plaster of Paris are mixed in equal parts, making sure that the plaster is fully suspended and that no air bubbles are trapped in the mixture (it is best to add plaster to water while continually stirring slowly). The liquid is then gently poured into the mould that has been placed around the imprint, being careful not to disturb the substrate.

The best moulds can be made from plastic tubing, cut into rings of different heights and diameters: a great use for all those discarded washing-up-liquid bottles. Allow thirty minutes for the plaster to dry, longer if the weather is damp or cold. Lift the mould gently and allow it to dry further before cleaning its surface under water with a soft brush. Removed from the mould you now have the perfect plastercast. To obtain an exact copy of the original print, the cast can be covered with a thin layer of vaseline or detergent, placed back in the mould and the procedure repeated giving you a positive and a negative matching pair.

An alternative to being encumbered with messy plaster of Paris is to carry a small sheet of perspex which can then be laid over the imprint and the track drawn with a felt-tip pen (and later transferred to a sketchpad or notebook as a lifesize illustration). This method was originally devised for recording the individually identifiable pug marks of Indian tigers and so the perspex sheet has been given the name 'tiger-tracer'.

A Longworth small mammal live trap baited and set.

Setting a trap

Essential equipment for the small mammal detective is the 'Longworth' live trap (see the address list at the end of the book for suppliers). This allows the capture and identification of mice, voles and shrews (and occasionally weasels) and is a very effective way to determine which species are present in a particular area. The Longworth trap is made of two parts, a tunnel entrance with trap door and tripping mechanism and a nestbox for food and bedding material, which are important to ensure the small mammal remains alive. Shrews in particular need to feed every 2-3 hours so a source of insect food must be provided (8g per trap of mealworms, maggots or blowfly pupae) and the traps should be visited frequently – at least twice a day, early morning and late afternoon (see Mammals and the law).

Successful trapping will depend upon where and how traps are placed, so anyone contemplating using them should read the excellent booklet on the subject published by the Mammal Society (see The mammal detective's library).

For the capture of other larger mammal species for the purposes of scientific study or control, a whole series of different sized cage traps have been designed. These, together with other methods such as netting or tranquillizing, require special licensing and even training that will not be available to the amateur mammal detective.

Another way to make elusive mammals accessible to you is through the use of nestboxes. In particular purpose-made dormice and bat boxes. The success of these depends on how and where they are sited but remember, as soon as they are occupied, you will require a special licence from the statutory Nature Conservation Organization in order to examine the contents (see Mammals and the law). All of the British bats, apart from the two horseshoe species, may turn up in the

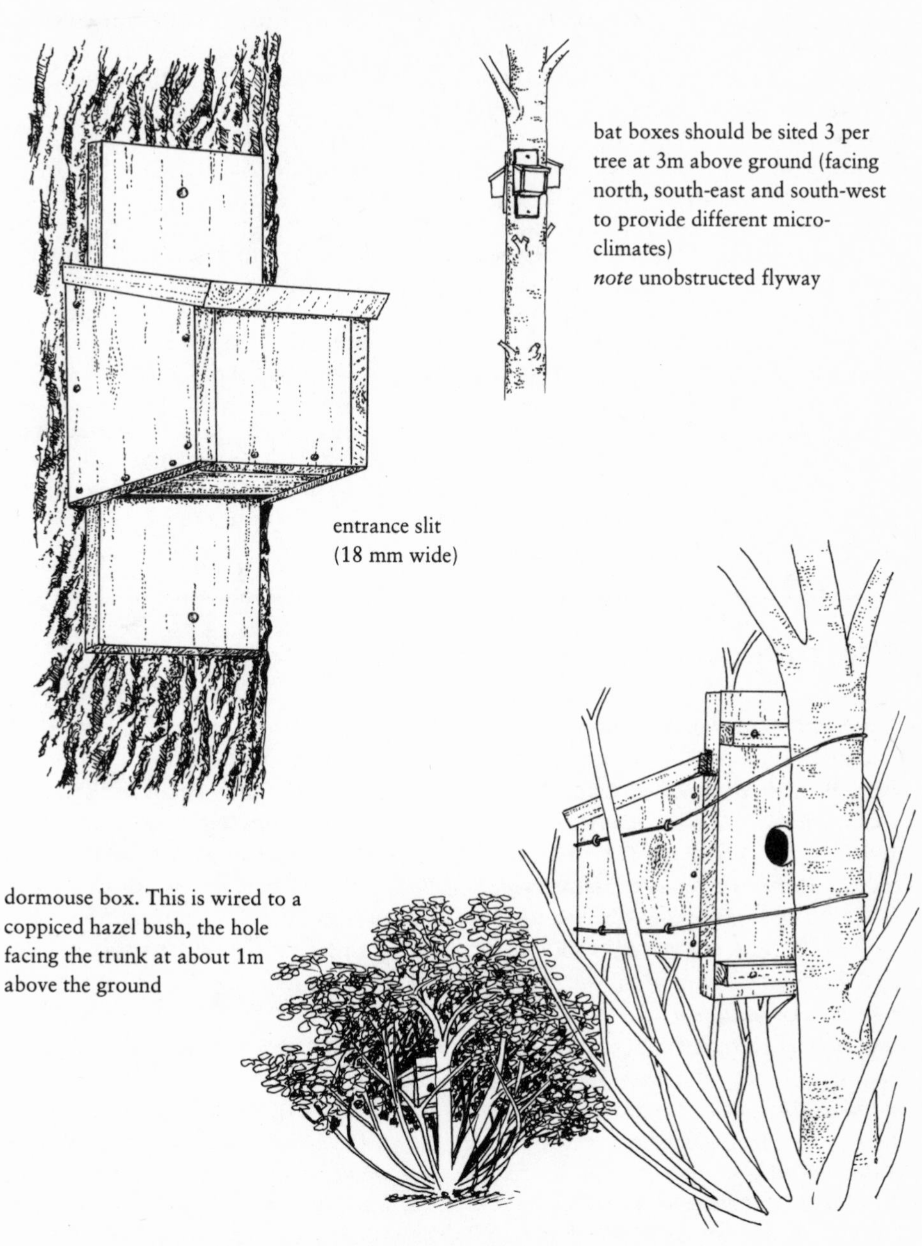

How to site bat boxes and dormouse boxes

standard bat box, sometimes in big numbers. The record currently stands at 65 brown long-eared bats in a single box (quite a handful to count while balanced at the top of a ladder I can tell you). Dormice have been found in some bat boxes, whilst yellow-necked mice, woodmice and even weasels have been encountered in dormice boxes. So checking the boxes can sometimes be pretty exciting, especially if wasps have moved in and built a nest, as I know to my cost.

Stake-outs, baits and bait-marking

For a prolonged period of surveillance the use of a hide or high seat will allow the mammal detective a certain amount of comfort. Alternatively, sitting in the branches of a tree may conceal you from the animals as well as allowing your scent to be carried above their heads. Stake-outs are best at breeding nests or burrows but an area may be baited with food to attract them in. This can work really well with some of the scavenging species such as fox and badger.

By placing small pieces of coloured plastic among a small pile of peanuts outside a badger sett, a subsequent search of the boundary latrines will show where they have been deposited. Using different coloured plastics at different setts, the mammal detective can determine the boundaries (and therefore the territory sizes) of the different clans of badgers.

Effective small mammal trapping

The small mammal detective can obtain a great deal of information about the small mammal populations under investigation by using 20, 30 or more Longworth traps laid out 10 metres apart in a square, rectangular or triangular grid. This system will provide good scientific data on which species are present and the relative numbers of individuals when comparing different sites or looking at the changes in the small mammal populations over several trapping periods (by using the same trap pattern and procedures.)

Each captured mouse, vole or shrew can be identified, weighed and examined for sex, age and breeding condition (the juveniles are recognized, not only because they are smaller and weigh less, but they tend to show a greyer and duller coat).

In order to handle the animal, the closed trap should be opened in a large, strong, polythene bag. Usually the bedding will need to be tipped out of the nest box to reveal what has been caught. You may be able to identify it straight away, but further examination needs to be done in the hand. Isolate the animal in one of the bag corners, while the trap and bedding are removed. Then slide your hand over its back to pinch the scruff

of the neck lightly between finger and thumb (this takes a lot of practice to gain confidence). Do not attempt to pick a mouse up by the tip of its tail, as the skin can be pulled off. Extracting the animal by the scruff, it can be further supported by holding the base of the tail with the other hand while you examine its underside.

Mark and recapture: *before release the small mammal can also be individually marked by a simple fur clip. Using fine scissors the tips of the guard hairs can be cut to reveal the darker hair base and underfur. Different animals may be clipped in different places on the body in different combinations. For instance, one may be marked right shoulder only, another right shoulder and right rump or left shoulder, right flank and so on. This allows these small mammals to be recognized on subsequent recapture in the session. The fur clip will last for about 2 or 3 weeks before it grows back. It is unlikely that all the animals in the population will be captured but an estimate of abundance can be made by using the mark-recapture formula at the end of the session:*

$$p = \frac{N + R}{R} \times M \quad \text{where}$$

p = population estimate
M= total individuals marked
R= total recaptured on that day
N= total new, unmarked

However, in practice most mammal detectives simply use the total of new animals caught over the sampling period (the minimum number alive - MNA) as a measure of population size. The MNA can be used when the animals caught at the end of the trapping period consist of mainly recaptures rather than new ones.

The trapping results also allow you to follow the movements of marked individuals over the trapping grid as they are re-caught in different traps on different days. This is particularly useful if you have trapped for a period of 10 days or more and the grid is quite large. The movements between traps can be plotted out on graph paper (especially if you have devised a square grid at 10 m interval spacings between traps) and the outermost trap positions joined up to create a convex

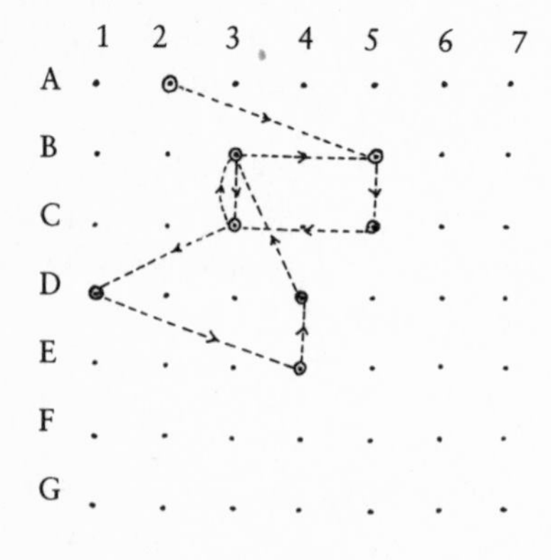

(1) Trap revealed movement of a marked individual

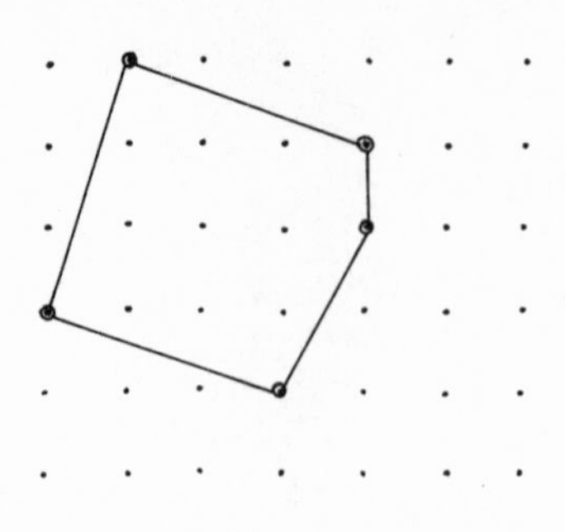

(2) Home range shown as a convex polygon of the same animal.

Examples of results of trapping with a 7 x 7 grid, showing (1) movement and (2) home range of a marked animal.

polygon. The area can then be calculated by counting the squares of the graph paper to produce an estimate of home range size, known as the minimum area convex polygon (see illustration). The home range size will vary between males and females, summer and winter and in different habitats. For example compare the home range estimates in the table below:

species	***season***	***habitat***	***home range size (m^2)***	
			males	*females*
woodmouse	*summer*	*dediduous wood*	*8,000*	*4,000*
	winter	*deciduous wood*	*2,000*	*1,800*
	summer	*arable*	*12,000*	*6,000*
bank vole	*summer*	*deciduous wood*	*900*	*300*
	winter	*deciduous wood*	*380*	*260*
field vole	*summer*	*grassland*	*500*	*300*
pygmy shrew	*summer*	*grassland*	*1,500*	*1,500*

High-tech surveillance: listening in the dark

An essential gadget for the mammal detective who has a passion for some of our least studied mammals is the tunable mini bat detector (see address list for suppliers). This transforms the ultrasound pulses emitted by echolocating bats down the frequency range to an audible wave band, allowing a human to hear the pattern of sound pulses. With experience the fine tuning allows the user to recognize the majority of the bat species by the differing frequencies, pattern and rate of sound. Listening in the dark to the passage of bats and counting feeding 'buzzes' – the sound like blowing a raspberry, produced by the rapid acceleration of sound pulses as the bat homes in on a flying insect prey such as a mosquito, moth or flying beetle – is fascinating.

Towards dawn the detector can be used to distinguish those bats feeding and those commuting back to their roosts which may be located by the distinctive sight and sound of bats 'swarming' outside the entrance. This is particularly useful in finding tree roosts in dark woodlands. The bat detector sounds like a Geiger counter near radioactivity. The bats can be followed travelling along a watercourse, woodland edge or tree-line directly to the roost, since they arrive back one after the other along the same route. When they reach the roost they circle close to the entrance point, sometimes 'swarming' in large numbers if it is a maternity roost, each bat flying back and forth to the entrance point many times before entering. A spectacular sight in the increasing light of dawn. Alternatively, by noting the direction of the path taken it is possible to backtrack along the line of commuting bats at dusk to their source and thus to their roost site. This process may need to be repeated over several evenings. Why not join your local bat group and get the hang of this with training from the experts? You can find their addresses from your local county wildlife trust or from the Bat Conservation Trust (see p. 126).

Surveillance cameras

For the really ambitious mammal detective who has access to the equipment, remote video cameras can be set up out in the open at feeding or breeding sites. These can then be linked directly to a TV monitor in the home for live surveillance or taped for later watching. This idea has led to some highly successful live TV programmes, 'fox watch', 'badger watch', 'bat watch' and 'night watch'. Remember that if you intend to film at the places of shelter used by any of the protected species, you will require a special licence to do so (see chapter on Mammals and the law).

Using stills cameras mounted on tripods at baits or nests, you can lie in wait some distance away, perhaps in a camouflaged hide, and set the camera off with a remote cable release. Another approach is passive, not requiring anyone to be present, the camera being activated by the animal itself setting off some form of trigger. This could be by breaking a beam of light, setting off an infra-red detector or a bat detector (or even a sound activated sensor). These camera traps could be left out along mammal runs and pathways or bat flyways to take one-off photographs of the passing animals. A power winder and use of flashguns mean that the camera can be left in place to take picture after picture until the film is used. For large or heavy animals a pressure pad concealed under the chosen path can enable the photographer to select only those mammals heavy enough to trigger the pad. This method has been successfully used in the rain-forests of South America and Asia to photograph some of the elusive big cats such as the jaguar and clouded leopard, but it would be equally useful for badgers or deer in Britain.

Using multiple flashgun exposure, the sequential movement of the mammal can be examined in the photograph. This allows actions too quick to be seen by the eye to be studied in detail. Bat researchers are using this technique so they can study the evasive manoeuvres used by some species of moth and lacewing insect to avoid being eaten by bats, an action that would normally be over in a split second.

Bugging and radiotelemetry

Another technique is a must for the serious mammal researcher who wishes to find out more about the behaviour, home range use (territory size) and places of refuge used by the mammal under study. This is radio-telemetry (radio-tracking), where the animal is first captured and then fitted with a small radio transmitter (known as a 'tag' which should be less than 10% of its body weight and is normally only 3-5%). This usually takes the form of a neck collar or shoulder harness, but is simply glued to the fur of bats and small mammals (or to the tail of moles!). With seals and cetaceans the transmitter is fitted as a cap on the head or back, the big whales carrying big and sophisticated tags.This procedure may require a licence from the Home Office if the attachment of the tag requires the animal to be put under recovery anaesthesia for safe handling or if the tag is going to be surgically implanted (Animals Scientific Procedures Act 1986). A separate research licence is also required if the species under investigation is one protected under the Wildlife and Countryside Act (see Mammals and the law).

In Britain, mammal detectives must operate their radio-tracking within the frequency waveband specifically allocated for use with wildlife radio tags (173-174 MHz), each tag tuned to a specific 2-3 kHz band between this range.

When attached and switched on, the radio gives off a signal at a set frequency wavelength. This sounds like a regular blip or bleep at a rate of around one per second (between 30-80 times a minute, depending on setting and battery strength). The bleeping signal can only be heard by tuning into the correct frequency wave band with a radio receiver and directional aerial. The subject can then be located by directing the aerial towards the strongest signal. With several receivers at work the triangulation of 'radio-fixes' can give the precise location at any one moment. The variation in signal strength can be interpreted as stationary or travelling behaviour, so the animal's activity can be easily recorded. During the day the constant signal will allow the sleeping places of nocturnal mammals to be exactly

Radio-tags are worn as collars, harnesses or glued on to those animals where the conventional collar is not suitable.

located. In one study of pine martens, some surprising and unexpected dens were found this way, including one cheeky animal that slept in the stick-pile eyrie of a golden eagle, a raptor that often kills martens.

I found it an invaluable experience to assist with radio-tracking of both pine martens and otters to learn how these animals use their respective habitats, where they would visit and what they would use as places of shelter. A pine marten could disappear down a hole under a tree root that was smaller than my clenched fist and an otter could curl up and vanish into a grass tussock. I was amazed at how little cover these animals could use to be hidden from view and this made me totally re-think where I should be looking for them.

Most radio telemetry is carried out by following the tagged animal using a portable radio-receiver and hand-held aerial, sometimes having to run to try and stay within range of the transmitter. However, semi-permanent receivers and aerials can be set up as constant monitoring stations. These are attached to tape recorders or electronic data loggers, allowing the investigator to be elsewhere (such as at home asleep!).

The radio tags are designed to fall off after a given period of time (collars and harnesses have degradable rivets, while glued on micro-tags can be groomed off as the hair grows underneath). Alternatively, animals may be recaptured and the tag removed or replaced. The technology is improving all the time, with tags not only becoming smaller and lighter but having increased performance over greater distances and a greater life span. Even the tiny bat-tags may now last for three months, allowing them to be easily located and retrieved when they fall off. Collars designed for mammals such as foxes and deer may now give a consistant tracking performance lasting two years, whereas the large cetacean tags have been designed for remote tracking by satellite and may still be working after ten or more years. These will allow the oceanic migrations of whales and dolphins to be followed and special sensors incorporated into the tags will collect information on heart-rate, breathing or temperature as well as recording the dive length and depth reached.

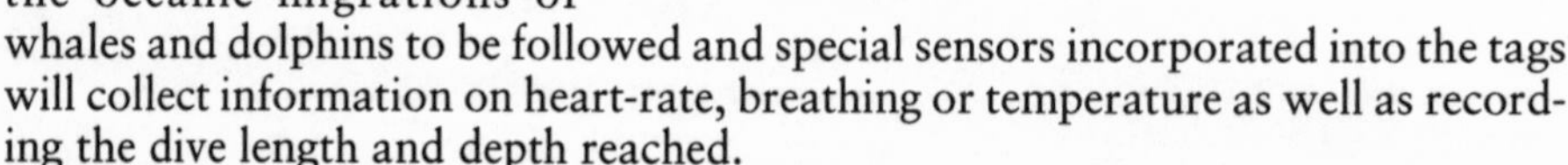

This high-tech surveillance method means that normally elusive mammals can now be located in the field and observed, but even with a bleeping 'bug' attached telling you that the animal is just in front of you, some species, particularly stoats, polecats and pine martens, may still be difficult to see since they spend so much time in dense cover.

Nevertheless, radio-tracking has revolutionized the study of all mammals and must be the most significant advance for the modern mammal detective.

Forensics

The forensic mammalogist
One area of detective work that requires specialist knowledge is that of forensics – the identification of the whole from the part (a fragment of material evidence). The forensic mammalogist is much more at home in the laboratory than out in the field but a hand lens and ruler are just as useful as a microscope and calipers.

Skulls and old bones Teeth, skulls and limb bones are the main skeletal material that can be successfully examined and measured in order to identify what mammal they came from. Indeed classification of most of the mammal families is based on the type and number of teeth present. Examination of the teeth may also tell you about the animal's life-style and what it fed on.
For identification of skulls, teeth and bones, see pp. 106-110.

Owl pellets The owl is a supreme mammal hunter – specializing in small rodents and shrews – providing the mammal detective with a ready sample of the small mammal community by way of its regurgitated pellets that may accumulate in vast numbers under favoured roost sites.

Seal skull: note unspecialized teeth for holding and biting fish.

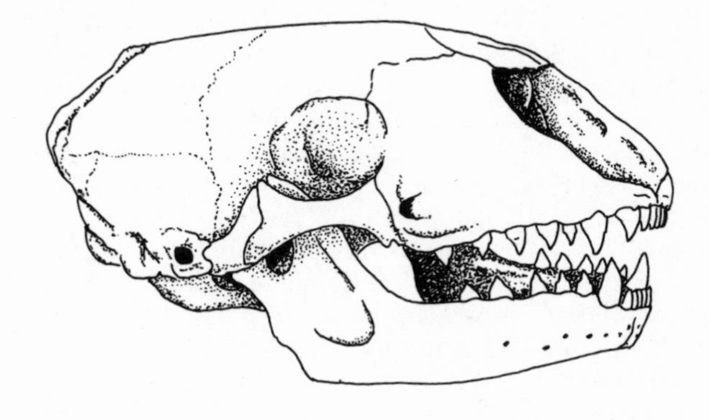

grey seal tooth

common seal tooth (note many lobed)

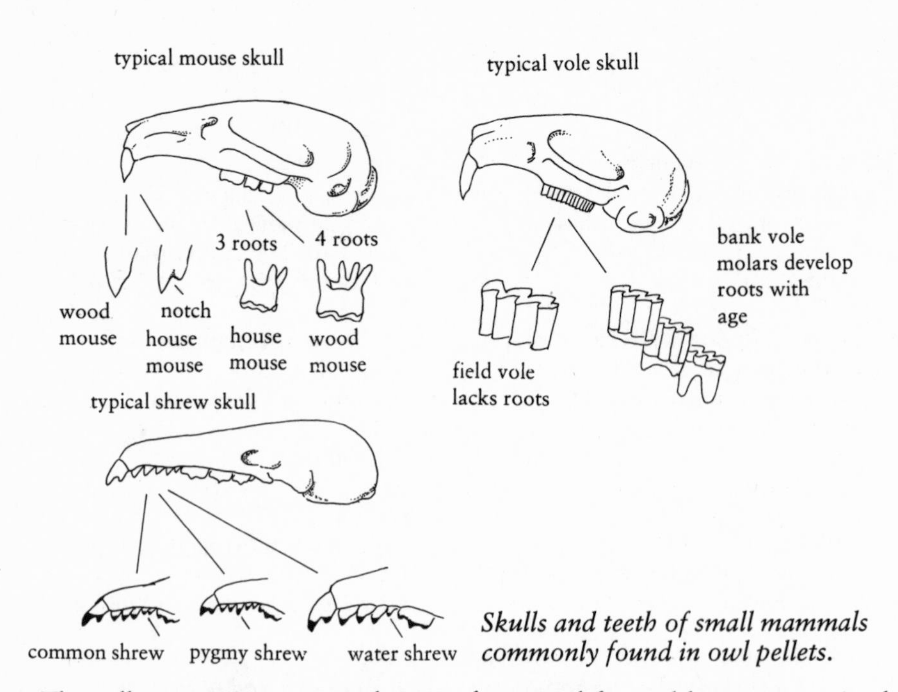

Skulls and teeth of small mammals commonly found in owl pellets.

The pellet comprises a matted mass of mammal fur and bones conveniently packaged into a tight pellet for easy collection. By collecting the pellets over monthly periods the seasonal changes in the small mammal community may be observed by their comparative frequency in the pellet sample. Of course some species may be more easily caught than others and so bias their proportion in the owl's diet but nevertheless it is a good way to find out what small mammals are around and may show the presence of less common species which would be difficult to find by small scale 'Longworth' trapping.

An owl produces one or two pellets every night and these are most likely to be found beneath regular roosts or nest sites. Of the British owls, the barn owl tends to be the most faithful to its roost sites and here very large samples of pellets may be collected. The tawny owl tends to leave its pellets scattered under a number of trees throughout its home range and so these are more difficult to collect. Short-eared and long-eared owls have favoured roosts where pellets of these less common species can be found, but, particularly with the short-eared owl, they may be left out in the open and more exposed to weathering. Little owls eat fewer mammals so the pellets tend to contain a lot of insect remains.

Other birds such as herons, gulls, crows and diurnal birds of prey also regurgitate pellets which may be of interest. However, eagles, buzzards, hawks and falcons all tend to rip their prey apart and often remove the head before consumption and their digestion may be so thorough that the bones disappear entirely. Owls usually swallow their prey whole and just digest the flesh, providing a more useful pellet for examination.

Dissecting owl pellets

It is best to work on the pellets one at a time as there is more chance of finding all the significant remains.

Soak the pellet for a few hours in warm soapy water to soften the hair mass or matrix (this also drives out any insect larvae that may be eating the sample). Place the now sodden pellet on newspaper and gently tease apart with forceps and needles. The matrix of fur will indicate mammal prey even if no bones are present, whereas a matrix of feathers will alert you to look out for bird bones. Skulls are very obvious and those that are intact will be the prize of the sample. Any lower jaws and teeth will help confirm identification. If there are no skulls present identification of the mammals may be possible from the larger limb bones.

It often helps to arrange the skulls and bones on a piece of black card. This may allow you to match up what belongs to what and you will soon learn to recognize the different parts of the skeleton. For more information I recommend that you read *The Analysis of Owl Pellets*, a very useful booklet published by the Mammal Society.

The use of owl pellets

1 Changes in the mammal composition in the diet of barn owls due to the removal of vegetation cover.

Water voles were found in 3% of the pellets examined from a roost beside a well vegetated waterway in Yorkshire prior to the cutting and clearance of reeds but comprised 28% afterwards.

At another site a rough meadow was regularly hunted by barn owls whose pellets showed field voles in over 60% of cases, but after a period of heavy over-grazing by horses the pellets revealed field voles in only 30%.

2 Changes in the mammal composition in the diet of barn owls as an environmental monitor:

At a regular barn owl roost in Durham pellets were collected each year throughout the 1980s. The owl hunted a small watercourse regularly where the water vole was a favoured prey being identified from about 25% of each year's samples of pellets until 1986 when it occurred in fewer of the samples. This coincided with the first mink being sighted on the watercourse. By 1989 and subsequent years less than 1% of the owl pellets revealed water voles, suggesting a dramatic crash in the local water vole population.

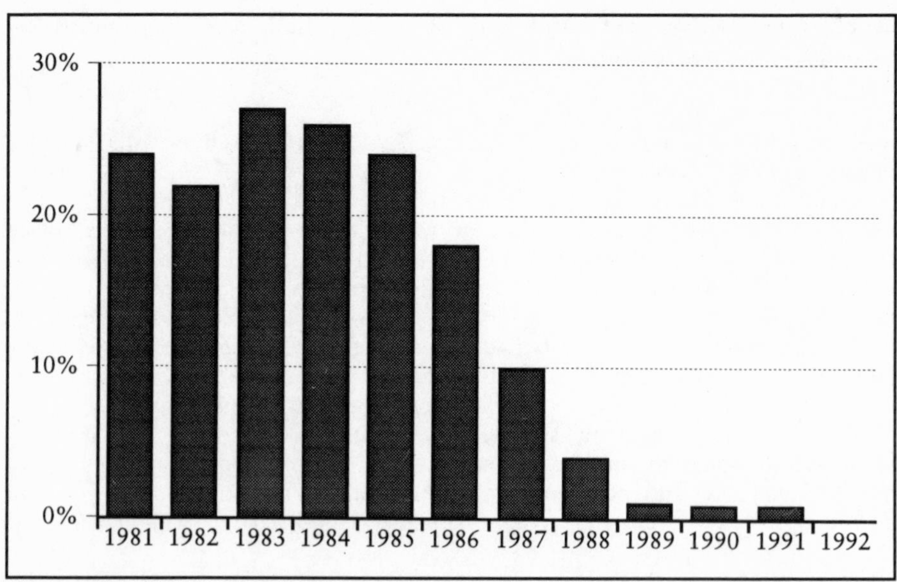

Owl pellets as an environmental monitor: frequency of water voles in barn owl diet (Co. Durham, 1981-92)

What the cat brought in

Domestic cats are another source of small mammal samples, usually brought back to the house as a small furry dead present dropped on the doorstep or on the carpet (if the cat has access to a cat flap). Sometimes the mammal will be entire and easily identifiable but more often than not the cat has made a meal of it and only the feet, tail or head remains.

Depending on the type of hunting ground and to some extent the size of the cat, these prey remains will range in size from tiny pygmy shrews to full grown rabbits.

The mammal detective, by careful examination of the remains, should be able to determine correctly which species has been caught. The most likely species are :

Commonly caught: common shrew, field vole, bank vole, woodmouse, house mouse

Less commonly caught: pygmy shrew, water shrew, yellow-necked mouse, rat, water vole, mole, baby rabbit

Rarely caught: harvest mouse, dormouse, weasel, bats (usually pipistrelle and brown long-eared), squirrel

While I was living in Durham over a ten-year period, our cat successfully caught and brought to me the third and fourth records of the water shrew in the county (a very under recorded species).

Diet of mammalian predators

The forensic mammalogist can spend many happy hours sifting through heaps of droppings to determine the diet of the study species. Indeed there are now numerous specialist guides to help tackle the subject ranging from the analysis of otter spraint and an atlas of mammalian hair to a guide to the analysis of bat droppings (see Mammal detective's library).

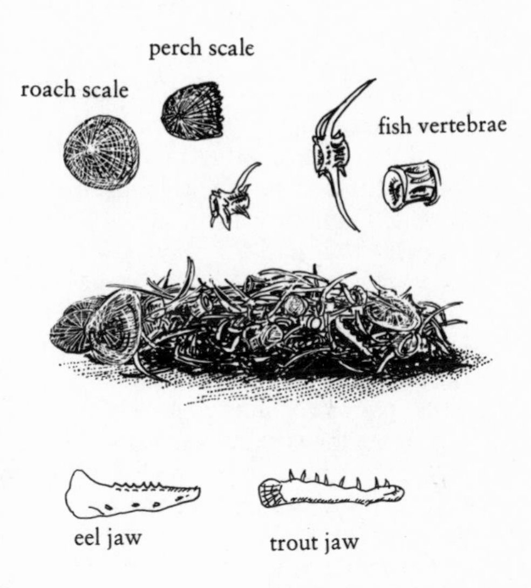

Otter spraint and fish bones.

It is best to start with some easily collected and identified droppings that contain relatively large fragments of material for identification. **Otter** spraint best fits this criterion, being easily located on ledges and rocks beneath bridges and generally contains vertebrae, bones and scales of fish, frog, crayfish or more rarely bird/small mammal. Coastal otters can show an even more diverse diet that changes with the seasons since they also crunch crabs and take a number of migratory fish species.

Fox scats, **mink** scats and droppings from other mustelids (best collected from outside dens) also provide fragments of easily identifiable material together with hair of their mammalian prey species (usually rodent or rabbit).

Badger dung pits yield plenty of dung to sift through, although it is often an amorphous mass of finely chewed material with plenty of mud in the sample. This is because the badger just loves to slurp up earthworms by the thousand and all that remains after digestion is the mud from the worm's gut and a few worm bristles (chaetae). The omnivorous badger may also eat carrion, fruit, seeds, grain, bulbs, rodents, birds and even hedgehogs, remains of all of which may be found in the dung pits.

For the really dedicated forensic mammalogist the task of examining **bat** droppings under a microscope can be most rewarding but the fragments can be very finely chewed in some species. As a rule the larger the bat, the larger the insect taken and the larger the fragments in the dropping (mind you I did hear about one pipistrelle that decided to tackle a poplar hawkmoth that was almost as big as itself – the saying 'eyes bigger than belly' springs to mind). With the dropping fragments spread across a glass slide, the task is to systematically search through the individual fragments under a microscope (low magnification) until some portion is found to be intact, standing out from the mass of undefined portions of chitinous fragments. This may be a complete beetle antenna, leg, a portion of wing or moth scales. These can be compared to pictures in an insect field guide.

Diet of herbivores

Mammals such as **deer, rabbits, hares** and many of the **rodents** digest their plant food very thoroughly so that the droppings contain such fine particles of plant material that is difficult to identify. Microscopic examination may reveal characteristic features of some special groups of plants that have curiously shaped hairs or stomata from the leaf surface or perhaps intact pollen grains (identifiable) from any flowers that had been eaten.

Most diet studies of herbivores are done by direct observation together with the identification of plant remains they leave behind.

As an incidental part of the Water Vole Survey of Britain 1989-90, I was able to identify plants from the material left by the water vole at its favoured feeding stations, platforms along the water's edge. This way I was able to note which plant species the vole fed on in its various habitats and throughout its range over mainland Britain: an amazing list of 227 plant species was compiled over the two years of the survey – one of the most comprehensive species lists to date for the water vole, but I'm sure it can be improved upon since not all habitats could be visited in all seasons with their accompanying change in available plant species.

For the budding forensic mammal detective the field of mammalian diet may still lead to some exciting new discoveries.

Take care when handling any mammal droppings since they may harbour disease (especially leptospirosis) or harmful fungal spores and even be a source of endoparasite infection (roundworm, etc.). Use disposable gloves and wash hands thoroughly.

Microscopic examination of mammal hair

Whether strands of hair found in the field (such as on barbed wire) or mammal hair in droppings or owl pellets, their examination under a light-microscope for their surface-scale pattern can help in specific identification.

A mammal's coat is composed of several types of hair: long stiff overhairs, known as guard hairs, and shorter, thin and wavy underhair. Although the underhair is the predominant type of hair in a coat, the guardhairs give the best clues in helping to identify the species. The clues are provided by the colour, form and length of the hair and its structure (the appearance of the scaled surface – the *cuticula* – and the hair's pith – the *medulla*).

With a light-microscope the pattern of the cellular structure of the medulla can be used to aid identification; however the shape of the cuticular scales on the hair's surface are difficult to see without special preparation. This problem is solved by making a gelatin impression of the hair on a microscope slide that reveals the scale pattern. To do this, dissolve a few granules of gelatin (enough will stick to the hairs of a fine, wet paintbrush) in 1cc of warm water (about a thimbleful). Paint a thin film on a microscope slide and allow to cool for ten minutes.

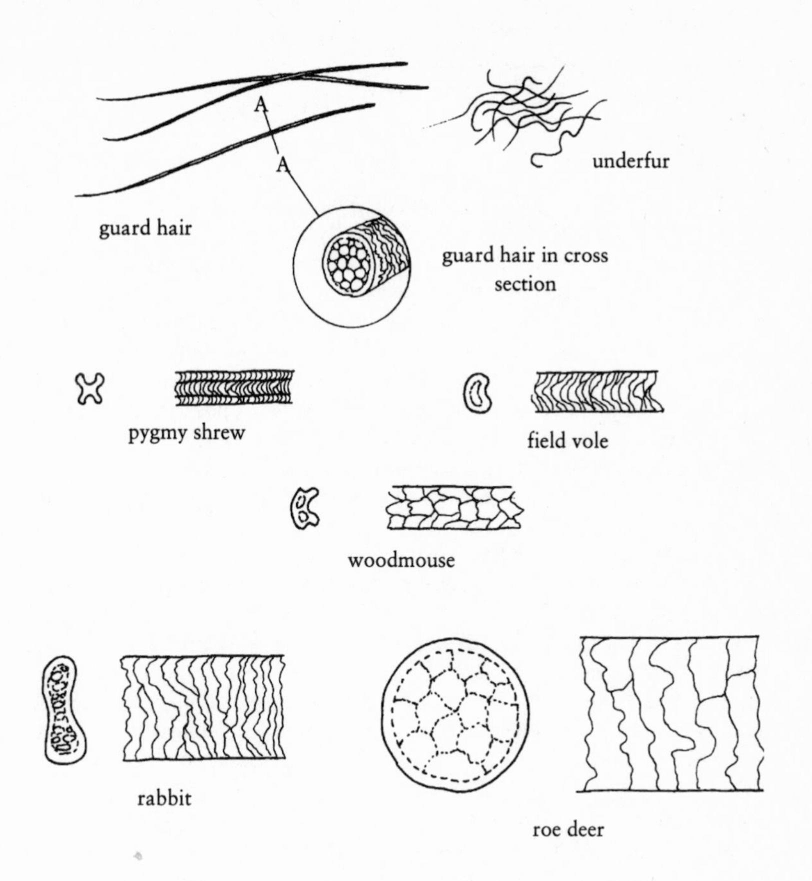

*(*Above*)Identification of mammal hair and (*below*) examples of different mammal guard hairs, showing surface scale patterns and cross-sections (all much magnified).*

Place a few hairs across the film with tweezers and leave for a further 30 minutes for the gelatin to harden. With great care gently peel the hairs off one by one and view under a microscope at x400 magnification to see the surface scale imprint.

The shape and dimension of the hair in cross-section is another important feature for hair identification and range from the simple cylinder to complex ridges and grooves that help trap air for insulation (these are most easily seen among the shrew species and so can be readily identified).

Mystery mammals

Exotic escapees

Always be prepared for the unexpected: escaped pets or mammals freed from private collections (deliberately or accidentally). This may provide some real detective work, tracking down reports of something really exciting, like the infamous 'beast of Exmoor', a notorious black panther, or similar big cat.

A friend of mine once encountered two chinchillas bouncing about a picnic site. Both were rounded up and now live happily in their new home; whether they would have survived in the wild one can only speculate (as they certainly bred in their new home). But the funny-looking rabbit tracks they left behind would certainly have given the mammal detective paws for thought!

A number of escaped exotics have enhanced the British mammal list by breeding in the wild, such as the muntjac deer or grey squirrel. Most notable are the American mink, coypu and muskrat which have been escaping from fur farms since the 1920s, to establish extensive populations in the wild. The latter two were responsible for a lot of damage to crops and were eradicated following expensive trapping campaigns. An estimated 200,000 coypu were at large in East Anglia in the 1960s but by 1989 the last individual was captured. The heyday for the muskrat was earlier in the 1930s when 4,500 were exterminated in a short campaign lasting three years. The last wild muskrat was trapped in 1937. Both of these aquatic rodents thrived in extensive wetlands feeding on marsh plants; they left large five-toed webbed footprints in the mud and what looked like massive water vole droppings. In the 1970s I found such signs myself among the coastal reedbeds of Suffolk. I particularly remember the large coypu droppings which were about 7 centimetres (3 inches) long, torpedo-shaped with curious narrow ridges which ran their length. I also found the runs and huge burrows, 20 centimetres (8 inches) across, in the ditches made by this large South American animal. Yet when I first saw one I thought I was watching a short-legged terrier dog until I noticed the long scaly tail!

With the change in fashion and the reduced demand for fur, nutria (coypu) and musquash (muskrat) are no longer farmed in Britain and the number of licensed mink farms has declined from about 700 in 1960 to less than 50 in 1994.

Smaller rodents have also escaped captivity to breed in the wild and there have been several reported colonies of Mongolian gerbils and golden hamsters. One group of hamsters successfully burrowed out of a shop basement and tunnelled under the street pavement to freedom, like prisoners of war!

The best documented colony of gerbils existed in burrows in and around a wood yard, under sheds and houses on the Isle of Wight. The population included over 100 animals in 1976, all descendants of a few gerbils used in a children's TV programme and left behind in 1973! Elsewhere several smaller colonies have

Coypu droppings (actual size) have distinctive furrows and are torpedo shaped.

established themselves under floors in houses and outbuildings, in gardens and occasionally in woodland. One mammal detective examining long-eared owl pellets collected in Yorkshire was amazed to find gerbil remains among the usual voles, mice and shrews.

Another rodent, the pretty dark-eyed, furry-tailed West Indian mouse, occasionally reaches Britain from the West Indies with the cargoes of bananas that are part of their diet but so far they have not established any breeding colonies at the docks or ports.

Crested and Himalayan porcupines, Canadian beaver, raccoons and wild boar have all managed to escape into the British countryside and breed, but as yet the populations have been very short lived, disappearing without further trace (unless you know different and have tracked some down!).

During the Otter Survey of England 1991-4, I received reports of a small population of Asian short-clawed otters living free on the river Thames system around the City of Oxford. Despite intensive searching I failed to locate any tracks of these animals but I did track down two specimens that were killed on the road in the area in 1983 and 1989. A photograph taken by a local resident showed a family group of four animals together, suggesting breeding in the wild. Their origins are still unknown and the case is still open.

On a birding trip to watch the passage of seabirds off the Cornish coast during August 1992, a friend reported watching the bobbing head of a seal through the telescope. Somehow it didn't look quite right. The animal then came ashore on a small rocky island and declared itself to be a Steller's sealion. Where it had come from nobody knows but it was certainly a long way from the rest of its species in the North Pacific Ocean. It always pays to keep an open mind and be prepared for the unusual and sometimes totally unexpected.

The case of the mysterious black beasts of Britain and other curious cat records

Over the years there have been an increasing number of 'big black cat' stories from many parts of Britain – glimpsed sightings, mysterious footprints and even allegedly savaged livestock. Some have become legendary, with many reported incidents; over 200 sightings of such a big black cat or cats have been logged for South West England alone. At the time of writing the most recent was dubbed the 'Beast of Bodmin' following evidence from two sources, one photographic and one camcorder,

from October 1993 and January 1994, that showed a large black leopard. Reports from Devon in 1993 led to the discovery by local mammal detectives of a deer carcass halfway up a tree, a typical leopard kill.

In 1980 a puma was caught near Loch Ness, Scotland, in a blaze of publicity. This famous cat, nicknamed Felicity, later died in captivity of natural causes and can now be found as a mounted exhibit in the Inverness Museum.

An animal shot in mistake for a fox, while it was raiding a chicken coup on the Isle of Wight during the winter of 1993, proved to be an escaped African serval. Another medium-sized spotted cat, a leopard cat, was shot by a Devon farmer in 1988 and that year one more was shot near Jedburgh, Scotland. Two years later another was found dead in the same Scottish county.

In 1988 a cat knocked down and killed by a car on Hayling Island in Hampshire was identified as an Asian jungle cat. A dead specimen of this species was also found the following year in Ludlow, Shropshire.

The mystery as to the origins of many of these exotic feline predators remains unsolved. How many more are surviving in the British countryside and whether any can become established as wild breeding species only time will tell ...

Mammals and the law

Complex legislation in Britain helps keep wild mammals free from being killed, harmed or disturbed by people. Different species fall into different categories that cover conservation, closed seasons or pest control, as well as provisions on the grounds of animal welfare and responsibility for wild animals in captivity. It also restrains the release of harmful and non-native species. The law is subject to change from time to time following reviews, and anyone wishing to rely on a point of law should consult the relevant Wildlife Act and its most recent amendments.

The Wildlife and Countryside Act 1981 (amended 1988) provides full protection for the species of mammal listed in schedule 5. These are: all **cetaceans, walrus, otter, pine marten, wildcat, red squirrel, hazel dormouse** and all **bats.**

This means it is against the law to:

- Kill, injure, capture or keep them (even for a short time for examination, species determination, or scientific marking for release without a licence).
- Disturb them in their breeding sites and places of shelter. Disturbing does not refer just to touching or moving the animals, but also to photographing them or doing anything that alarms them or rouses them from hibernation.
- Destroy or damage their breeding sites or places of shelter, or obstruct the ways in and out of them. This provision does not apply to dwelling houses except in the case of bats in non-living areas of the house such as the loft space. (There have been several successful prosecutions for killing bats or damaging their roosts in the lofts of houses during the course of timber treatment. Such work can be carried out legally following a letter of advice from the Statutory Nature Conservation Organization.)
- It is also an offence to sell, barter or exchange a schedule 5 mammal whether dead or alive (or any part or derivative thereof) without relevant licences and documentation. The onus will be on the person in possession to prove the specimen was obtained legitimately.

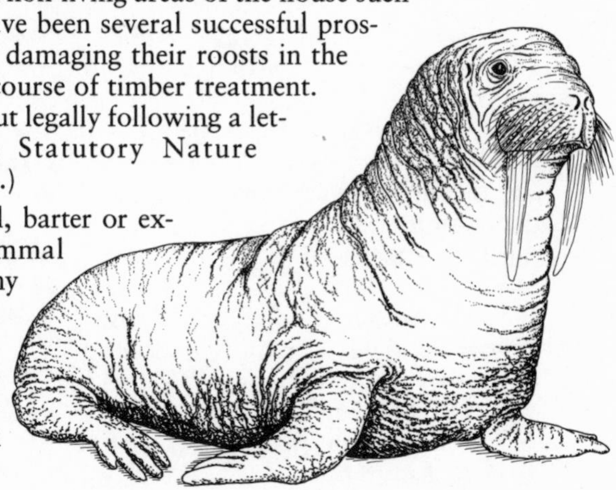

The walrus is a surprising addition to Schedule 5 of the Wildlife and Countryside Act 1981.

Although **badgers** are not rare or endangered, the Badger Act 1973 (amended by the Wildlife and Countryside Act and a later

1992 Badger Act) provides them with the same protection as a schedule 5 species, except where there is a need for licensed control of numbers, such as in places where an outbreak of Bovine Tuberculosis has occurred. The sett is protected while the animals are occupying it and under the amendments any person accused of attempting to or actually killing, injuring or taking a badger or digging at a sett is presumed to be doing so illegally unless it can be proved otherwise.

The accidental killing or injury of a protected species is not a breach of the law, such as accidentally running over an otter with a car. It is also permissible to keep and take care of any injured protected species until it can fend for itself again. Where possible the animal should be released as close to where it was found (very important in the case of bats). If the animal is too badly hurt to recover, it may be humanely killed without breaking the law (it's best to take it to a vet).

Although it is not against the law to kill or capture mammals that are not fully protected there are strict regulations regarding the methods that may be used or there may be restrictions as to the months of the year in which it is legal to do so.

Schedule 6 of the Wildlife and Countryside Act lists the species that have prohibited methods of killing or capture. This schedule includes all those on Schedule 5, plus **badger, fat dormouse, hedgehog, polecat** and **shrews** (all species).

Those listed must not be caught or killed in traps or snares except under special licence that permits the use of certain types of free-running snare or cage trap which must be inspected at least once a day. For **shrews** an open general licence can be obtained for the use of Longworth small mammal traps.

Seals are fully protected during their respective breeding seasons (Conservation and Seals Act 1970 + amendments). The Deer Acts (1959, 1963) invoke a close season on the shooting (culling) of **red, sika, fallow** and **roe deer**.

Non-indigenous species of mammal are prohibited for release into the wild and any such animal that attains pest status can be controlled. Schedule 9 of the Wildlife and Countryside Act lists the following species: coypu, fat dormouse, gerbil, prairie dog, American mink, porcupine, black rat, grey squirrel.

The maximum fine for anyone intentionally breaking the law is £2,000; if more than one animal is involved, each offence can be dealt with separately. A sobering thought for anyone intending to destroy a bat roost of 100 or more individuals!

Licences are issued for the scientific study of protected species. These are needed in order to check bat boxes or dormouse nestboxes and handle the occupants. They may be granted by the Statuatory Nature Conservation Organization (see p. 126) in order to photograph, capture, handle or disturb certain specified mammal species following acceptance of an application form supported by referees or completion of training as in the case of the bat roost visitor's licence.

Licences for the control of protected species that are found damaging livestock or crops or in order to preserve public health and safety are granted by government agricultural departments.

The fleeting glimpse

It is rare to get a good long, close view of most of our British wild animals; often it's only a fleeting glimpse of a tail disappearing into the undergrowth or something streaking across the road or on the verge as we whizz by in the car.

This chapter will help you use the features you saw to solve the mystery of identification.

Size and colour are important elements in the identification of all wild animals. Try to compare the proportions of the animal seen with a familiar species such as a domestic cat and note its main colour and any markings. Ask yourself, were there any spots or stripes; was there a throat patch? facial pattern, tail or rump patch? were the legs long or short? was the tail bushy?

Other clues can be gained from its posture or the way it moved (its 'jizz'); what it was doing (before it was startled into fleeing), and where it was seen. If possible a subsequent search around the area where the animal was seen may reveal other tell-tale signs (footprints or droppings – see later chapters) to help confirm your identification.

Antlers compared (note that Chinese water deer does not grow any antlers).

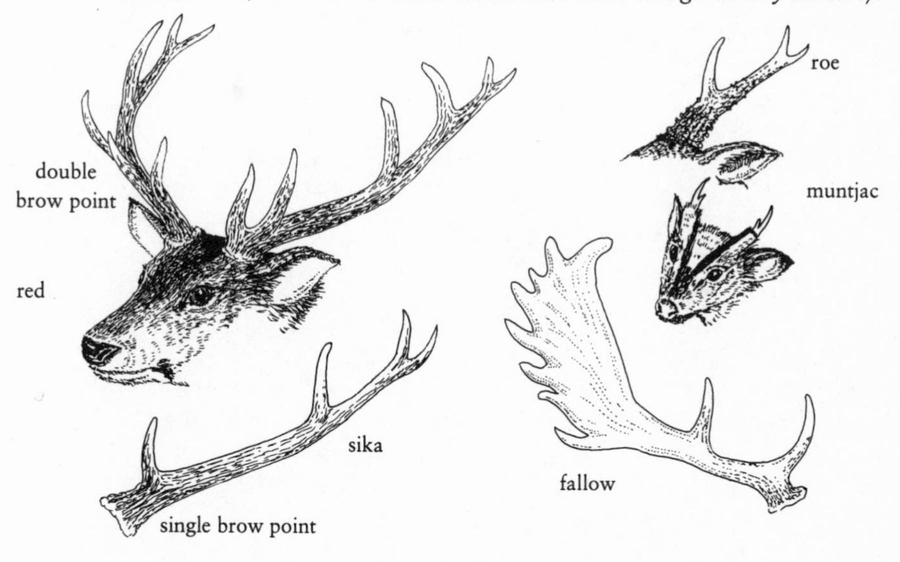

Can eyeshine be used to identify different species of mammals at night ?

The retina at the back of the eye is made up of special cells on to which the light is focused. Some mammals, such as ruminants (cows, sheep and deer), and most carnivores, have an additional layer of reflective cells behind the retina (known as the tapetum) that throw light back as a bright eyeshine when the mammal's pupil is enlarged at night. The reflected colour will depend on whether it is looking straight at the light source or at 90° to it due to refraction. The eyes look green, blue, orange or red. However, with experience and using other clues such as where the head is in relation to the ground, the mammal detective can make some educated guesses at an animal's identity. For instance, red deer eyeshine tends to be green; that of sheep also tends to be green, but the upright head of the red deer is much higher off the ground (unless the sheep is standing on a mound!). The fox normally shows orange eyeshine, whereas a cat's eyes reflect green and a pine marten is a vivid electric blue. The eyes of an otter glow like dull red coals since its thick cornea is adapted to an aquatic environment, the same is also true for seals.

Rabbits, hares and rodents lack the tapetal layer but do reflect an eyeshine from the actual colour of the retina (an orange or red).

This is an area that the amateur mammal detective may like to investigate further; no field guide yet has discussed the eyeshine of mammals as an identification aid.

Identity parades

Use the series of identity parades that are based on annotated comparative drawings to help you crack the true identity of the animal you saw. The shadow outlines of Labrador dog or cat give relative shape and size. Accompanying information includes distinguishing features, calls, alternative names and species that look similar.

THE UNMISTAKEABLES

Some species need no introduction; these are

FOX
Aliases: red fox, vixen, tod, reynard
Giveaways: erect ears, slender muzzle, long bushy tail with a white tip.
Call: far carrying scream during rut (enough to make your hair stand on end), triple bark or yelp.

BADGER
Aliases: brock, baget, bawson, grey pate, Billy
Giveaways: unmistakeable black-and-white striped face.
Call: variable from gruff bark to scream as well as 'whickering'

SEMI WILD PONY
Aliases: Fell pony, Dartmoor, Exmoor, Welsh, New Forest and Shetland ponies
Giveaways: bay or brown coloured with pale muzzle, thick coats, dark manes and swishing tails
Call: mostly silent, may 'whinny'

FERAL GOAT
Aliases: Billy goat
Giveaways: both sexes horned, long shaggy coat and beard
Call: bleats and nasal snorts

RED-NECKED WALLABY
Aliases: scrub or Bennett's wallaby
Giveaways: unmistakeable long tapering tail, upright stance, short forelimbs but long hindlimbs
Call: usually silent but may growl or hiss

HEDGEHOG
Aliases: hedgepig, tiggywig, urchin
Giveaways: unmistakeable spiny coat
Call: snuffling and huffing sounds

MOLE
Aliases: moldwarp, taupe, want
Giveaways: black, velvety fur and spade-like forelimbs
Call: silent

THE WHALES AND DOLPHINS

Of the 26 species that have been recorded in British waters, half of them have only ever been seen on very rare occasions, but 14 species can be described as regular and these are included here.

They can be grouped into different size categories (but this is always difficult to judge at sea) but the most important character that aids identification is the dorsal fin. The larger whales may also give a characteristic spout as they surface to breathe.

Choose from the following size categories and compare the shape, size and position of the dorsal fin. Note also any flank markings.

Small (up to 3m/9 ft long)

HARBOUR PORPOISE
Aliases: porpoise
Giveaways: small size with small triangular dorsal fin. Dark grey colour
Lookalikes: small dolphins, but note their sickle-shaped fins.

COMMON DOLPHIN
Giveaways: small swift dolphin with long slender beak. Yellow-and-white hourglass patch on flanks
Lookalikes: other small dolphins

STRIPED DOLPHIN
Aliases: Euphrosyne dolphin, blue-white dolphin
Giveaways: small swift dolphin with long slender beak. White V-shaped blaze on flanks
Lookalikes: other small dolphins

Medium (3-6m/9-18ft)

BOTTLE-NOSED DOLPHIN
Aliases: Flipper!
Giveaways: unmarked robust dolphin with short beak
Lookalikes: other medium sized dolphins

RISSO'S DOLPHIN
Aliases: none (scarface!)
Giveaways: robust with blunt head and tall sickle-shaped dorsal fin. Uniform grey with many white scars
Lookalikes: other medium sized dolphins

WHITE-SIDED DOLPHIN
Aliases: Atlantic white-sided
Giveaways: robust with short beak. White oval patch on flank behind dorsal fin
Lookalikes: other medium sized dolphins

WHITE-BEAKED DOLPHIN
Giveaways: stout grey dolphin with white short beak and whiteish patches on flanks and back. Large curved dorsal fin
Lookalikes: other medium sized dolphins especially white-sided. Dorsal fin resembles Risso's or killer whale's

Large (6-10m/18-30ft long)

KILLER WHALE
Aliases: orca, grampus
Giveaways: tall triangular dorsal fin in centre of back. Black with white patch behind eye and grey saddle behind dorsal fin
Lookalikes: distinctive dorsal fin but check Risso's, white-beaked and pilot whale

PILOT WHALE
Aliases: long-finned pilot whale, caaing whale, pothead whale and blackfish
Giveaways: long, slender flippers, low curved dorsal fin in centre of back, bulbous head, black colour
Lookalikes: killer whale, bottle-nosed whale

NORTHERN BOTTLE-NOSE WHALE
Aliases: bottle-nosed whale
Giveaways: upright curved fin two-thirds along length of back. Bulbous head. Dark coloured and large.
Lookalikes: minke whale, pilot whale, beaked whales

MINKE WHALE
Aliases: lesser rorqual
Giveaways: small curved fin two-thirds along length of back. Pointed snout and white bands on flippers.
Lookalikes: other large whales

Huge (10-25m/30-75ft long)

FIN WHALE
Aliases: common rorqual
Giveaways: huge back with tiny curved fin set two-thirds along. Pointed snout.
Lookalikes: other big whales (minke and sperm); note also possible vagrant species SEI WHALE and BLUE WHALE

SPERM WHALE
Aliases: none (Moby Dick)
Giveaways: huge square block-like head, no proper dorsal fin but a series of ridges along back near tail
Lookalikes: other large whales

HUMPBACK WHALE
Giveaways: rotund, barrel-shaped dark whale with white flippers, low dorsal fin, may breach.
Lookalikes: other large whales

dog for scale
bottle-nosed dolphin
beak
small triangular fin
no obvious marks
no beak
porpoise
yellow patch
beak
beak
flank
common dolphin
white-sided dolphin
blaze
beak
striped dolphin
dark flank
white-beaked dolphin
sickle-shaped fin
scars
blunt nose
tall fin
Risso's dolphin
white patch
killer whale

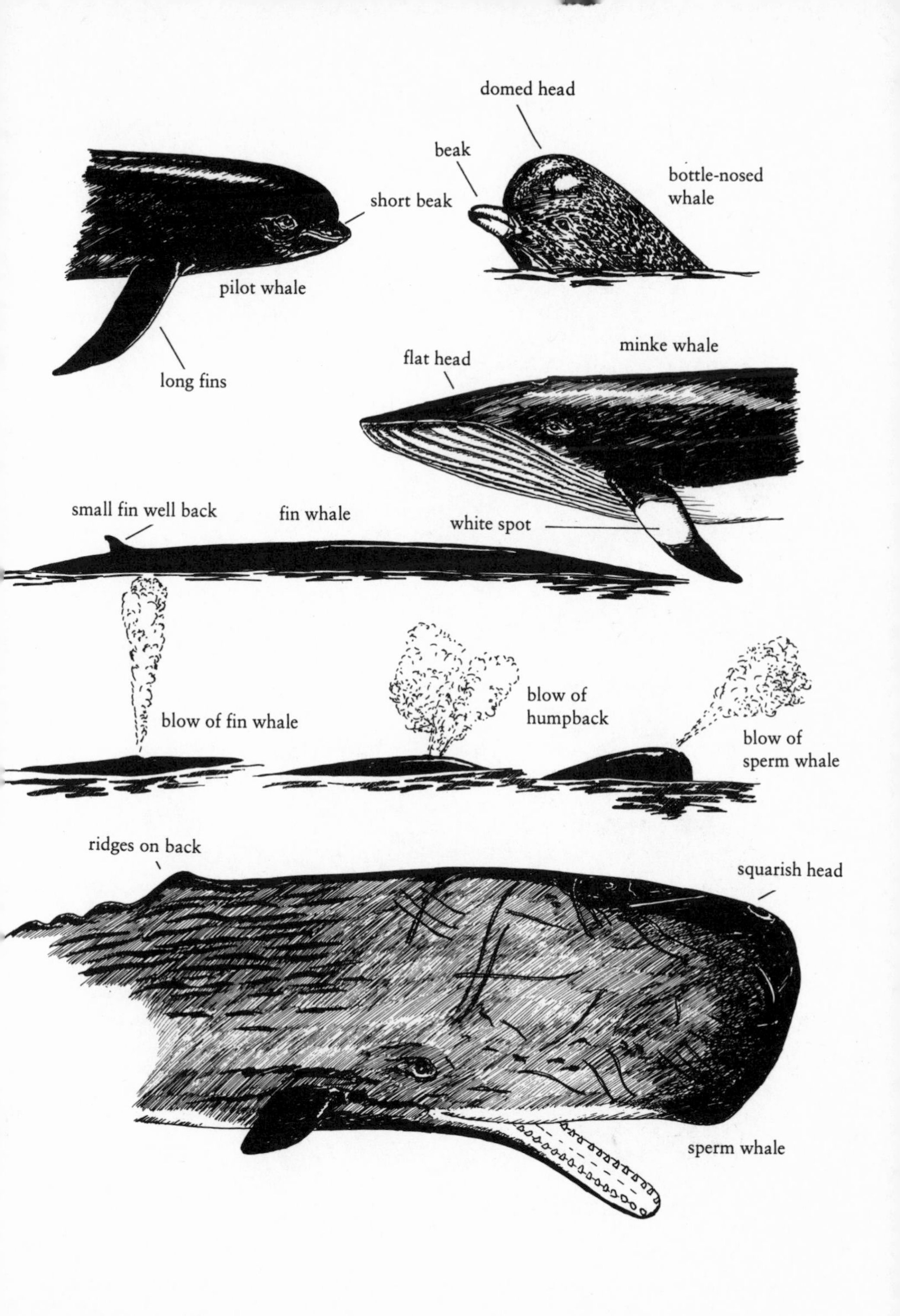
domed head
beak
bottle-nosed whale
short beak
pilot whale
long fins
flat head
minke whale
small fin well back
fin whale
white spot
blow of fin whale
blow of humpback
blow of sperm whale
ridges on back
squarish head
sperm whale

SEALS

Of the 7 species of pinnipeds that have been recorded in British waters only 2 breed here and can be regularly encountered.

COMMON SEAL
Aliases: harbour seal, sand seal, spotted seal, selchie
Giveaways: rounded head, V-shaped nostrils
Call: not very vocal, growling threats and snorts

GREY SEAL
Aliases: Atlantic seal, great seal, selchie
Giveaways: elongated head, parallel nostrils
Call: vocal, hiss, snarl, growls and moans

relative size and shape compared to Labrador dog

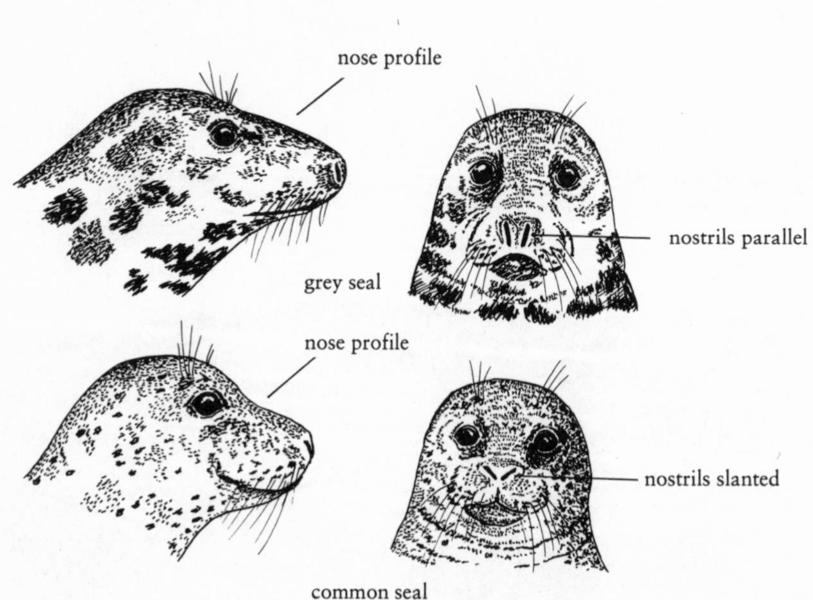

WILDCATS

It is quite difficult to differentiate the true wildcat from a large striped domestic cat just from appearance alone; interbreeding between the two confuses the issue further.

WILDCAT

Giveaways: large robust 'tabby', thick ringed tail that ends in a blunt tip

Call: mostly silent but spits and growls when threatened; wailing scream in fights and purring between mother and kittens

FERAL CAT

Aliases: tom, farm cat, pussy cat, alley cat, tiddles etc.

Giveaways: variable coat but tail tapers to a pointed end

Call: mostly silent, meow and wail in confrontation, purring

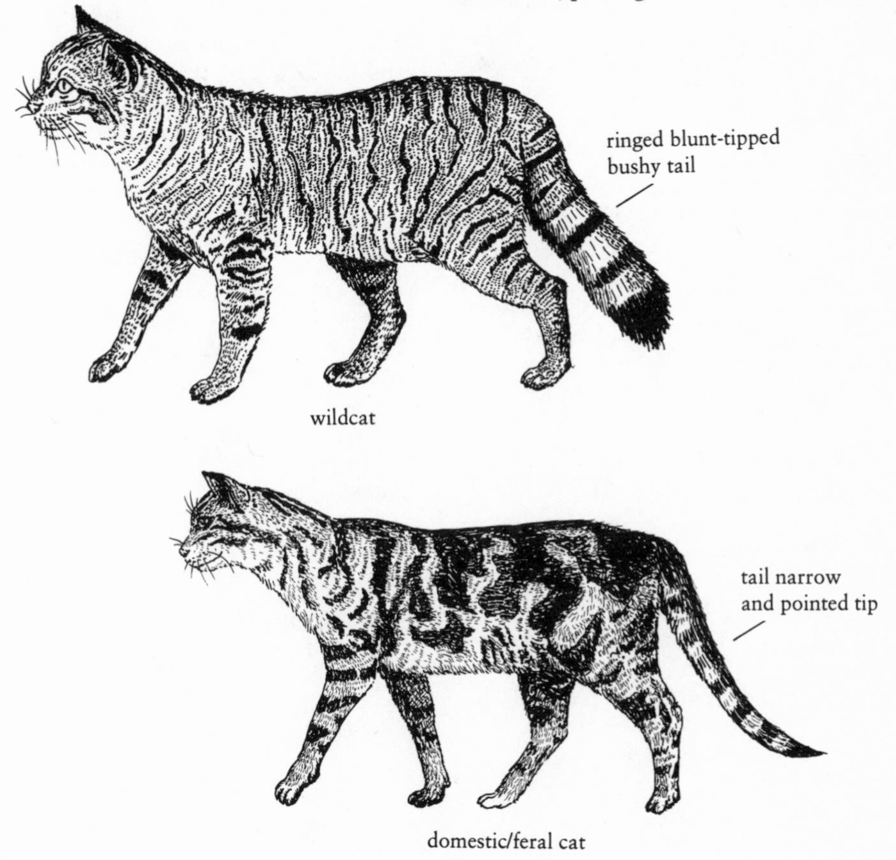

MUSTELIDS

OTTER
Aliases: water dog, cudoun, Tarka
Giveaways: flattened head-shape, long tapering tail
Call: a thin reedy whistle
Lookalikes: mink (but size difference)

PINE MARTEN
Aliases: marten cat, sweet mart, bele
Giveaways: pointed face, large rounded ears, pale throat patch, long fluffy tail
Call: solitary animals very quiet, family groups 'whicker' and may make huffing and growling noises when fighting or playing
Lookalikes: fox, mink, polecat and ferret (possibly red squirrel)

MINK
Aliases: none (Minnie the ...!)
Giveaways: long body, slightly bushy tail half body length. Generally dark colour, inquisitive
Call: normally silent but may shriek or hiss when attacked, family groups make 'chuckling' contact calls
Lookalikes: polecat, ferret, pine marten and possibly otter

POLECAT
Aliases: foul mart, fitch, hob and jill
Giveaways: bandit facial markings, cream coloured underfur below dark coat. Longish body, short legs, short furred tail
Call: normally silent but hiss and scream when threatened. Family groups 'chuckle and whicker'
Lookalikes: ferret, mink and pine marten

FERRET
Aliases: polecat ferret, fitchet, fitch, hob and jill
Giveaways: like a washed-out polecat
Call: as polecat
Lookalikes: polecat and its relatives

STOAT
Aliases: ermine, white weasel, royal hunter, clubtail, hob
Giveaways: long slender body, short legs, shortish tail with distinctive black tip. Reddish brown coat in summer, white in winter. Underside always white, inquisitive
Call: usually silent but hiss and shriek when threatened. During the mating season a high-pitched and excited 'squeaky gate' sound
Lookalikes: other small and medium sized mustelids

WEASEL
Aliases: grass weasel, mousehunter, rassel, kine, 'streaker'
Giveaways: very small, long and thin with short legs and tail that has no black tip, inquisitive
Call: as stoat, making a high-pitched trilling when excited
Lookalikes: stoat

comparative sizes of cat, otter and weasel
weasel
pale ears
pine marten
short tail
wavy flank
throat patch
long, bushy tail
black tail tip
stoat
straight flank
polecat
dark fur
distinct face mask
short, bushy tail
white chin
mink
indistinct face mask
ferret
pale fur
broad muzzle
buoyant mink
long, tapering tail
otter
otter swimming

DEER

Six species of deer occur in the British countryside.

Compare the proportion and build of each; note the differences in rump patch, tail length and the antler pattern if present. In summer some species have spotted coats and all are brighter and glossier than the dull thick winter ones.

RED DEER
Aliases: stag, hind
Giveaways: large non-spotted red-brown deer, creamy rump patch. Branched antlers in stag
Call: far carrying 'roar' of rutting stag, gruff alarm barks
Lookalikes: other large deer

SIKA DEER
Aliases: Japanese or jap deer
Giveaways: stocky deer with spotted coat, white tail, stag has branched antlers
Call: high pitched whistle of stag in rut and high pitched alarm bark
Lookalikes: red and fallow deer

FALLOW DEER
Aliases: spotted deer, hart
Giveaways: spotted coat and black tail, stag has large palmate antlers
Call: deep belching groans by stag in rut, short bark of alarm
Lookalikes: sika deer, but note tail

ROE DEER
Giveaways: smallish slender deer reddish brown coat with distinctive white rump patch. Buck has short pronged antlers
Call: short repeated barks
Lookalikes: other small deer

MUNTJAC
Aliases: Chinese muntjac, Reeves's muntjac, barking deer
Giveaways: small hunched deer, ridged brow and white tail flag. Buck has short simple antlers.
Call: loud single bark, often repeated. Can scream when alarmed
Lookalikes: roe and Chinese water deer in appearance and field sign

CHINESE WATER DEER
Aliases: water deer
Giveaways: long neck, wide rounded ears and protruding tusks. No antlers
Call: bark, whickering or whistle alarms
Lookalikes: roe deer and muntjac in appearance and field sign

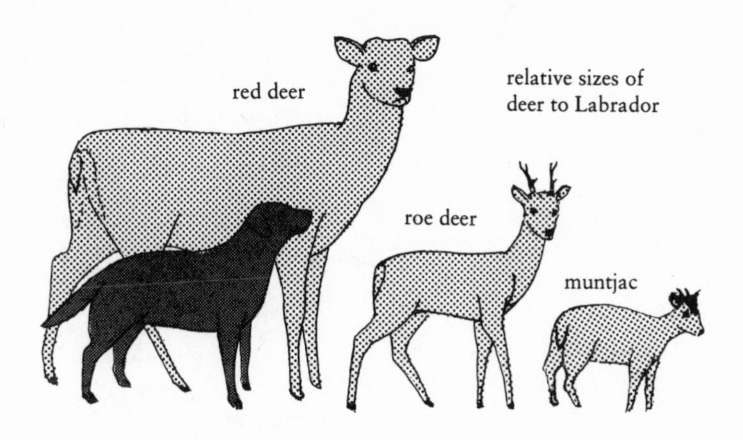
red deer
relative sizes of
deer to Labrador
roe deer
muntjac

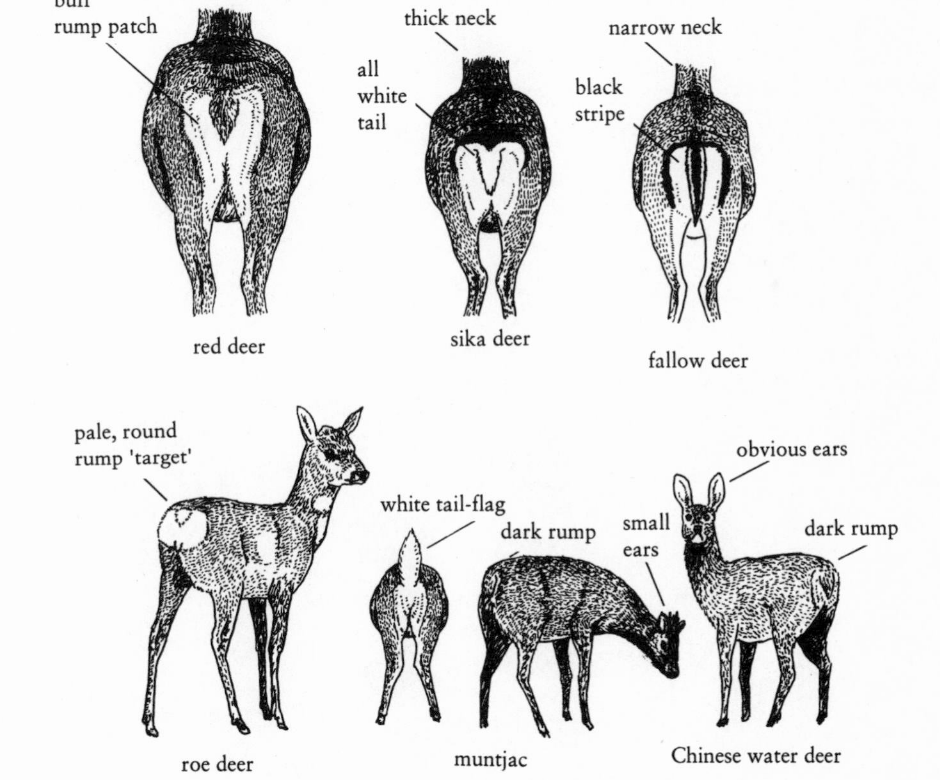
characteristic rump patches
buff
rump patch
thick neck
all
white
tail
narrow neck
black
stripe
red deer
sika deer
fallow deer
pale, round
rump 'target'
white tail-flag
dark rump
small
ears
obvious ears
dark rump
roe deer
muntjac
Chinese water deer

SQUIRRELS

RED SQUIRREL

Aliases: common squirrel, light-tailed squirrel, skug, tufty
Giveaways: dark colour, bushy tail, ear-tufts
Call: loud and soft chucking sounds
Lookalikes: grey squirrel

GREY SQUIRREL

Aliases: American grey squirrel, cat squirrel
Giveaways: grey grizzled coat, bushy tail
Call: various, including tooth chatter, kuk, lip-smacking and moan
Lookalikes: red squirrel and fat dormouse

FAT DORMOUSE

Aliases: edible dormouse, glis, seven-sleeper
Giveaways: small grey squirrel with bushy tail
Call: shriek similar to tawny owl chick
Lookalikes: grey squirrel

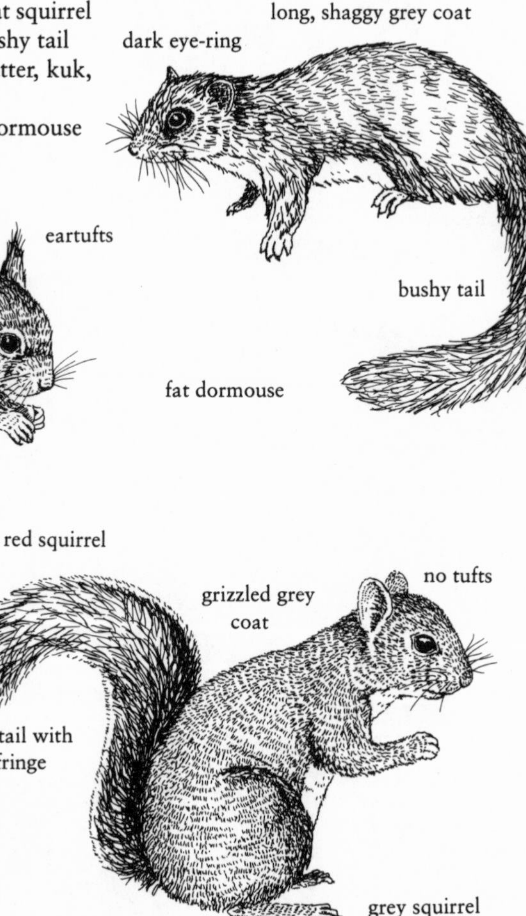

dark, bushy tail

eartufts

red-brown coat

red squirrel

RABBITS AND HARES

BROWN HARE
Aliases: common hare
Giveaways: long black-tipped ears, loping gait and short tail with black upperside
Call: normally silent but will squeal when attacked
Lookalikes: mountain hare and rabbit

MOUNTAIN HARE
Aliases: Irish hare, blue hare, Arctic hare
Giveaways: smaller, greyer than brown hare, turning white in winter
Call: usually silent
Lookalikes: brown hare and rabbit

RABBIT
Aliases: coney
Giveaways: smaller than hare, shorter ears without black tip. White tail flag
Call: silent but will squeal when attacked, foot is thumped as a warning
Lookalikes: hares

relative size of rabbit to cat

BATS

Fourteen species of bat are known to breed in Britain and another six species have occurred as vagrants in recent years.

Identifying bats in flight with any certainty is very difficult and it's not until the bat is seen close-up or examined in the hand that identification to species can be made. Some species can be readily distinguished by their size, shape, flight style and how they hold their wings at rest. Others need to be closely examined to look at the faces, ears and tail membranes together with measurements of the forearm.

Ultrasound calls may be distinguished with a bat detector.

GREATER HORSESHOE BAT

Giveaways: at rest wraps wings around body. Forearm 54-61 mm
Flight: hunts close to the ground over rough pasture, heathy hillsides and woodland edges. Slow butterfly-like flight with glides. May hunt flycatcher-style from perches.
Call: ultrasounds emitted through nostrils focused by noseleaf, therefore highly directional and strongest on the detector when the bat is flying directly towards you at close range.
Call is a constant frequency sound of a narrow frequency band and gives a very distinctive warbling on the bat detector at. 77 – 83 kHz
Lookalikes: unmistakeable at roost

LESSER HORSESHOE BAT

Giveaways: plum-sized bat, wraps wings around body.Forearm 37-42 mm
Flight: as greater horseshoe bat
Call: as greater horseshoe at 105 – 111 kHz
Lookalikes: none

NATTERER'S BAT

Giveaways: medium sized bat, pink membranes, ears separate, extending beyond muzzle, forearm 36-43 mm
Flight: hunts in woodland and wooded river valleys. Emerges late from roost often in near total darkness. Wingbeats slow, occasionally hovering, highly manoeuvrable in confined spaces.
Call: sound a rapid series of faint ticks without much variation over a broad range (40-110kHz) – best at 50kHz.
Lookalikes: Daubenton's, whiskered, Brandt's and long-eared bats
Related species are: GREATER MOUSE-EARED BAT, like a very large Natterer's but now extinct in Britain, and BECHSTEIN'S BAT, like a longer eared Natterer's, but restricted to a few counties in southern England

DAUBENTON'S BAT

Aliases: water bat
Giveaways: medium sized bat with large feet, forearm 35-41 mm
Flight: riparian species hunting over water. Flight fast, agile within 50 cm (20 ins) of water surface but also around trees.
Call: rapid pulses of sound, 'machine gun fire' (rat-tat-tat-tat) strongest at 45kHz
Lookalikes: Natterer's, whiskered, Brandt's

WHISKERED BAT
Aliases: Teesdale bat, bearded bat
Giveaways: small dark bat, shaggy coat, forearm 32-36 mm
Flight: hunts around vegetation, woodland edge and over flowing water in an agile weaving flight. Fluttering wingbeats often with glides.
Call: rapid dry clicks without the slaps of pipistrelles. Sounds are strongest at 45kHz.
Lookalikes: Brandt's bat, Daubenton's and pipistrelle

BRANDT'S BAT
Giveaways: as whiskered, but detailed examination in hand allows identification based on facial characteristics and membrane colour. Forearm 31-38 mm
Flight: as whiskered
Call: as whiskered
Lookalikes: whiskered, Daubenton's and pipistrelle

PIPISTRELLE
Aliases: common bat, house bat
Giveaways: small brown bat, forearm 28-35 mm
Flight: manoeuvrable flight often in a regular 'beat'. Woodland edge, around buildings, street lamps and over water.
Call: ultrasonic cry almost as loud as noctule with an audible social call at 20kHz (has the loudest voice for its size!) Fast sound like hard clapping (dwarfs applauding!) strongest at 45-55kHz
Lookalikes: other small bats, especially myotids
Related species have occurred as vagrants (check specialist books for more details) NATHUSIUS' PIPISTRELLE, KUHL'S PIPISTRELLE, SAVI'S PIPISTRELLE

NOCTULE
Aliases: great bat
Giveaways: long winged bat with sleek golden fur, forearm 47-58 mm.
Flight: can be seen flying high and fast often mingling with swifts and swallows and chasing the same prey. First seen about 15 minutes after sunset.
Call: ultrasounds emitted are so loud they are easily picked up on the bat detector at 250-300 metres (800-1,000 feet) distance and are audible to the unaided ear at 18-20kHz. Slow characteristic rhythm 'chip chop chip chop'.
Lookalikes: Leisler's and serotine

LEISLER'S BAT
Aliases: hairy-armed bat
Giveaways: as noctule but smaller and darker. Forearm 38-47 mm
Flight: as noctule
Call: emits at a higher frequency of 25-35 kHz
Lookalikes: noctule
Related species of similar size PARTI-COLOURED BAT that has bi-coloured fur and has been recorded as a vagrant from northern Europe

SEROTINE
Aliases: evening bat
Giveaways: large, robust brown bat, broad wings, forearm 48-57 mm
Flight: large bat like noctule but broader winged and different flight pattern – hawks close to ground or vegetation
Call: ultrasound range 20kHz tweet to 35kHz hard clap. Best heard at 27kHz as fast 'tap-dancing'
Lookalikes: other large bats in flight
Related species NORTHERN SEROTINE has turned up as a vagrant but is smaller

BROWN LONG-EARED BAT
Aliases: common long-eared bat
Giveaways: distinctive long rabbit-like ears, even in flight. Medium sized with broad wings. Forearm 34-42 mm
Flight: hunt amongst dense foliage of trees and shrubs often hovering to pick moths off leves or tree trunks
Call: long-eareds emit a weak fast pulse as a series of faint clicks on the detector at close range only – strongest at 50kHz
Lookalikes: Natterer's, Bechstein's and related species GREY LONG-EARED BAT which is restricted to a small part of the south coast of England and the Isle of Wight

BARBASTELLE
Giveaways: medium-sized very dark bat, with distinct squarish ears. Forearm 36-44 mm
Flight: as long-eared
Call: best detected at 32kHz as slightly harder castanet smacks
Lookalikes: none in hand, other medium bats in flight

flight styles of different bats compared: greater horseshoe (GH), noctule (N), serotine (S), pipstrelle (P), Daubenton's (D) and brown long-eared (LE)

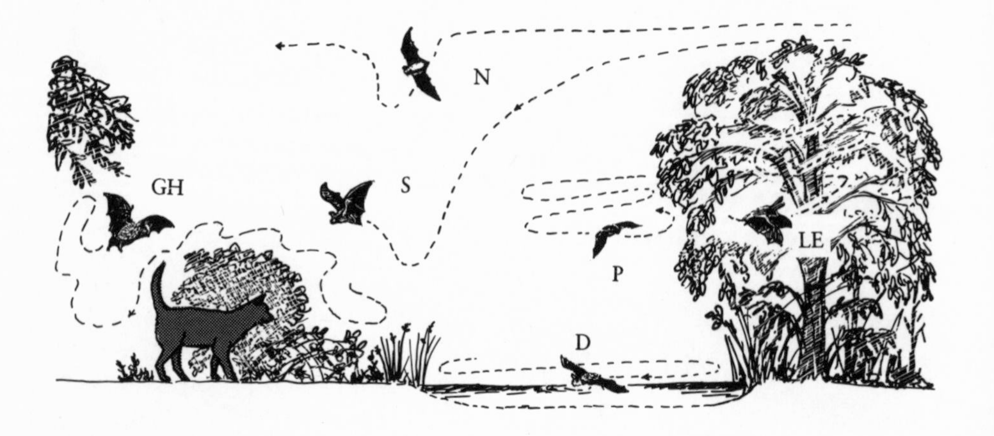

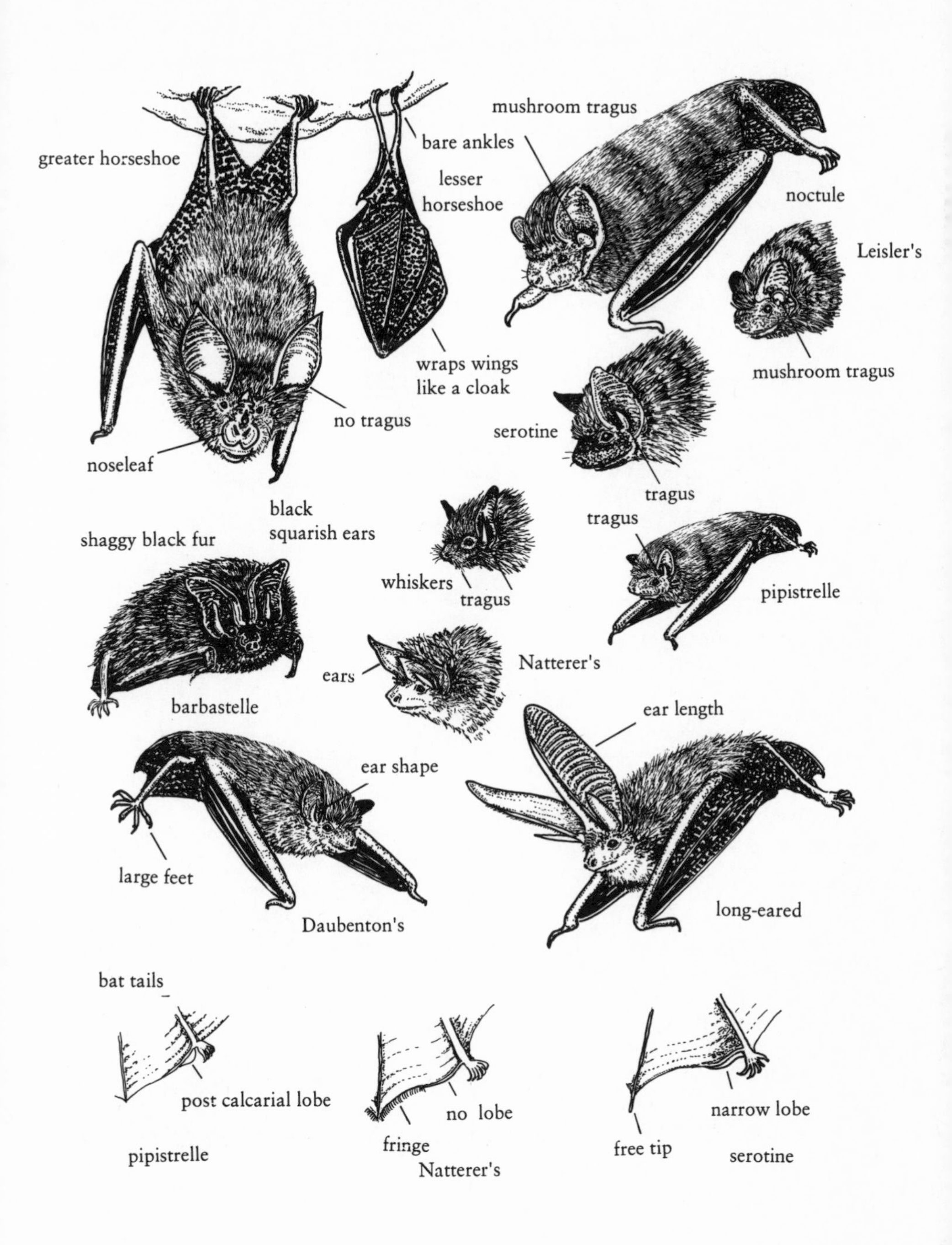
greater horseshoe
bare ankles
lesser horseshoe
mushroom tragus
noctule
Leisler's
mushroom tragus
wraps wings like a cloak
no tragus
noseleaf
serotine
tragus
black squarish ears
shaggy black fur
tragus
whiskers
tragus
pipistrelle
barbastelle
ears
Natterer's
ear length
ear shape
large feet
Daubenton's
long-eared
bat tails
post calcarial lobe
pipistrelle
no lobe
fringe
Natterer's
narrow lobe
free tip
serotine

SMALL MAMMALS

Which of the following descriptions best describes your sighting?

a	Tail heavily furred and fluffy. Roundish head shows large bulbous eyes and long whiskers. An agile climber.	➤ Dormice
b	Tail long, thick, sparsely furred and scaly. Rat sized with pointed muzzle, pronounced ears and bulbous eyes. Runs, jumps, climbs and swims well.	➤ Rats
c	Tail long, thin and sparsely furred. Mouse-sized with pointed muzzle, pronounced ears and big eyes. Hops and scurries.	➤ Mice
d	Tail short and well furred. Mouse- to small-rat sized with rounded muzzle, small eyes and ears buried in fur. Runs well or may swim and dive.	➤ Voles
e	Tail shortish with short fur. Small mouse sized to tiny with long pointed, twitching muzzle, tiny eyes and small ears. Frenzied movement.	➤ Shrews

This group comprises the similar looking smaller rodents and small insectivores. When trying to sort out which of these small mammals you saw, look at the shape of the muzzle, the size of the ears and the relative length of the tail when compared to that of the body.

HAZEL DORMOUSE
Aliases: common dormouse, sleeper
Giveaways: mouse sized with bushy tail, bright golden-brown colour
Call: silent but may make shrill squeaks when molested
Lookalikes: harvest mouse but much larger

BANK VOLE
Aliases: red-backed vole, wood vole
Giveaways: blunt nose, small eyes and ears, tail fairly long and well furred
Call: high-pitched squeak
Lookalikes: other voles and mice

FIELD VOLE
Aliases: short-tailed vole, short-tailed field mouse
Giveaways: as bank vole but shorter tail
Call: as bank vole
Lookalikes: other voles and mice. A slightly larger relative is found on the Orkney Islands ORKNEY VOLE

WATER VOLE
Aliases: water rat
Giveaways: like bank vole but much larger, swims and dives well
Call: mostly silent but shrill squeak when threatened
Lookalikes: brown rat and other voles

dormouse
large eyes
well furred tail
large ears
black rat
large ears
brown rat
hairless tail
short ears
well furred
tail
water
vole
harvest mouse
large ears
wood
mouse
short ears
field vole
short tail
prehensile tail
short ears
tail
length
yellow
collar
house mouse
bank vole
yellow-necked
mouse
thin tail

BROWN RAT
Aliases: common rat, Norway rat, sewer rat
Giveaways: pointed muzzle, pronounced ears and scaly tail
Call: shrill squeaks, 'grunt' squeaks and whistles
Lookalikes: water vole and BLACK RAT, a related species now confined to one or two islands, and very occasionally some docks.

HOUSE MOUSE
Aliases: grey mouse
Giveaways: pointed muzzle, small eyes and ears, tail long and scaly
Call: shrill squeaking
Lookalikes: other small rodents

WOODMOUSE
Aliases: long-tailed field mouse
Giveaways: protruding eyes, large ears and long tail
Call: high-pitched squeaks
Lookalikes: other mice

YELLOW-NECKED MOUSE
Giveaways: as woodmouse but yellow collar
Call: as woodmouse
Lookalikes: woodmouse

HARVEST MOUSE
Aliases: dwarf mouse, red mouse, red ranny
Giveaways: tiny mouse with prehensile tail, bluntish muzzle
Call: shrill squeaks
Lookalikes: other small mice

WATER SHREW
Aliases: otter shrew, water ranny
Giveaways: black dorsal fur, swims and dives well
Call: loud shrill rapid squeaking, also churring
Lookalikes: other shrew species, house mice

COMMON SHREW
Aliases: shrew mouse, ranny
Giveaways: brown shrew smaller than water shrew, long muzzle, frantic movement
Call: high-pitched, rapid 'chee-chee-chee'
Lookalikes: other shrews

PYGMY SHREW
Aliases: lesser shrew
Giveaways: tiny, small version of above
Call: very high-pitched chit, but often inaudible
Lookalikes: other shrews

Related species found only on the Isle of Scilly LESSER WHITE-TOOTHED SHREW, similar to common shrew, but has distinctive long hairs on tail.

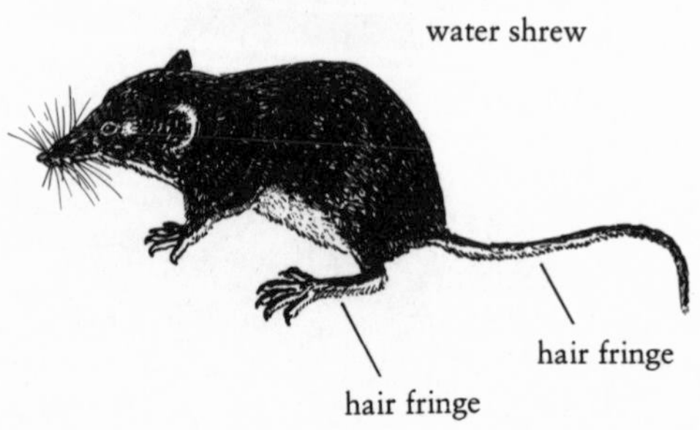

On the right track – a guide to mammal footprints and trails

There is nothing like a fall of heavy snow or chancing upon an expanse of fine silt to get the mammal detective excited. These conditions really reveal the tracks and trails of our terrestrial mammals and put the skills of the mammal detective to the test. Probably 90% of the tracks found by the observer are likely to have been made by the domestic animals and pets that surround us, so it's very important that the mammal detective knows what these look like first in order that they can be eliminated from the line of enquiry about those other different and more interesting looking footprints. With the eye 'tuned-in' the imprints left by our elusive native mammals can soon be spotted.

This chapter will help you use logical steps to sort out which animal was responsible for the tracks you have just found.

Remember to bear in mind the habitat and the likelihood of which species may occur there (but also keep an open mind at the same time: I once encountered a perfect clear set of otter tracks in a woodland that was some distance from the nearest river).

Types of footprint

There is an old country saying that goes 'the snow is the book of the soul'. This is because it is very easy to read the signs of animals and people in the snow; it reveals a clear impression of the animal's feet, and the structure of the foot in turn reveals a lot of information about the life-style of that animal. Mammals that move by running and jumping, such as deer, do so on the tips of their toes and have longer legs than those that amble along at a steady pace, such as the badger and hedgehog, which tread with the whole sole of the foot. Animals that are well adapted to swimming, such as the otter, have webbing between the toes that sometimes shows up in the imprint.

Broadly speaking mammal footprints can be divided into two main groups according to the structure of the foot (the hoof and the paw).

The imprints of hooved animals register as a single large toe print or two parallel slots (known as cleaves). Occasionally on soft ground or in snow, a second pair of marks appear behind the cleaves from the 'dew claws' that are positioned a little higher on the foot.

The imprints of non-hooved animals normally register as four or five toes arranged around a central pad made by the palm or sole of the foot (palmer pad). Claw marks may also be visible depending on whether the ground is hard or soft, but in some species such as cats the claws are retractile and are not normally seen.

Carefully interpreted, tracks provide the mammal detective with a reliable means of recognizing the mammal to species level without ever having to see the animal itself. However, in practice it is very rare to find a classic textbook example of a track and you will have to follow the trail as far as possible to get an idea of the range of impressions made by the animal, while trying to locate the best and most complete track and any other diagnostic field sign such as droppings. The set of tracks in a trail will also depend on how the animal had moved, that is, what its gait was. The position of the individual footprints vary in relation to one another depending on whether the animal was walking, trotting, galloping or bounding. You can read a great deal from good trails, being able to deduce when the animal was walking slowly, perhaps a carnivore stalking its prey, and where it had suddenly pounced or moved off in full chase.

What track and trail is it?

In order to identify correctly which species made the track in front of you it is first necessary to take some accurate measurements of the imprint and work out whether you are looking at the fore or hind foot. In almost all of the British mammals apart from the rodents the imprints of the fore feet are more distinct, being broader and deeper than those of the hind feet. They also tend to be more splayed, showing the toes more clearly. In dogs the palmer pad has a concave trailing edge, in the fore foot, but convex in the hind foot.

In measuring a footprint, the length is taken as from the front edge of the longest toe to the hind edge of the palmer pad in the fore foot or the heel in the hind foot. The claws are not normally included in the measurement. The width is usually taken as the distance to the edge of the outermost toes. Slow moving animals generally leave the best tracks for measurement whereas a running animal often slips and leaves a distorted print.

Use the question and answer key (on p. 82) based on measurements of the track and examine the series of life-sized and scaled drawings.

Deer The trails left by deer are essentially the same and will vary, depending on whether the animal was walking, trotting, galloping or jumping. When an animal is walking the footprints form two distinct and separate parallel rows. As the animal increases its pace from walk to trot to gallop the length of stride increases. When bounding or jumping the animal takes off with a powerful thrust of the hind legs and lands on the fore-limbs, the hind feet superimposing the foreprints or lying a little in front, giving a group of four tracks together. The cleaves of the fore foot are always widely splayed in a V when a deer jumps.

Seals Seal tracks are very characteristic and cannot be confused with any other animal track, consisting of pairs of shovel-shaped flipper marks either side of a broad drag mark from the body (the back flippers are not used in moving on land). The flipper marks may show 5 toes and claw marks (see illustration opposite).

Cats, dogs and foxes The track and trail of a wildcat is very similar and therefore very difficult to tell apart from a domestic cat or feral cat.

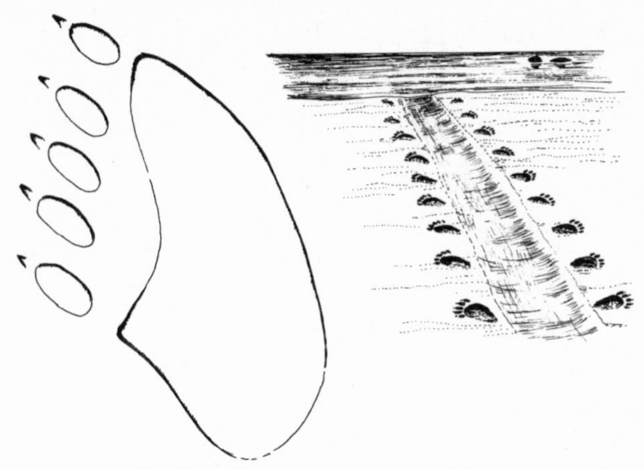

Seal tracks are unmistakeable.

In snow the tracks of a trotting cat lie in a straight line like those of a fox, the hind foot overprinting the fore foot.

The position of the toes helps distinguish between dog and fox (see illustration on p. 87). Dog tracks vary tremendously in size depending on breed but all show a similar track that is as broad as it is long with obvious thick blunt claws.

The trail of the trotting fox is fairly distinctive, following a purposeful course and showing a row of obliquely positioned pairs of footprints. This is because the animal trots with its body slightly at an angle to the position of travel. In a trot the stride length of the fox is about 50-70 centimetres (20-27 inches). Dog trails tend to be erratic with frequent pauses and changes of direction.

The mustelids Mustelids typically move in a bounding gait due to their long supple backs and powerful strongly angled hind legs (the exception being the ambling badger). The trail always shows paired or groups of three or four tracks since one or both hind feet may register in the tracks of the fore print.

In all species 5 toes may be seen on both fore and hind feet arranged in an arc around the central palmer pad. However, not all tracks will show the 5 toes clearly and often only 4 can be seen (compare the sizes of the annotated life-size illustrations on pp. 86-7).

The trail of the badger leaves a stride of half a metre with a wide straddle between left and right feet in its ambling gait.

However, badgers can move remarkably fast with the stride increasing to 80 centimetres (31 inches). I once surprised a badger in a conifer plantation late one afternoon when I suddenly came upon it walking along a forest path. The startled badger actually jumped vertically in the air, with all four feet leaving the ground before it galloped away in big leaps and bounds to clear fallen branches in the same way a deer would.

A KEY TO THE IDENTIFICATION OF MAMMAL TRACKS

Use the drawings to identify which species.

Q 1 a Is the track of a hoofed animal? ➤ Q 2
b Is the track of an animal with paws? ➤ Q 5

Mammals with hooves

Q 2 a Does the hoofprint show an almost circular track made by one toe? (12 centimetres/5 inches long, 12 centimetres/5 inches broad or bigger) ➤ pony or horse

b Does the hoofprint show two halves as slots always showing indentations made by the dew claws? ➤ Q 3

c Does the hoofprint show two slots without normally showing dew claws marks? ➤ Q 4

Q 3 a A large half-moon shape pair of cleaves with dew claw marks always present(8-9 centimetres/ 3-3.5 inches long, 9-10 centimetres/ 3.5-4 inches broad) ➤ reindeer

b Dew claw marks very obvious and lying out to the sides of the track. Front of cleaves rounded (5-6cm long) ➤ domestic pig/wild boar

Q 4 a Hoofprint rounded at front, dew claw marks never present. 5-12 centimetres(2-5 inches) ➤ sheep or goat

b Hoofprint pointed at front, dew claw marks visible where the animal jumped onto soft ground. 3-9 centimetres (1-3.5 inches) long. ➤ deer

Mammals with paws

Q 5 a Tracks large (c.20 centimetres/8 inches) and distinctive as paired 5-toed flippers either side of body drag marks ➤ seals

b Track up to 8 centimetres(3 inches) long showing 4 distinct toes on both fore and hind feet. The heel does not show as the animal walks on its toes ➤ cats, dogs and fox

c Track up to 6 centimetres (2 inches) long normally showing 5 distinct toes on both fore and hind feet ➤ mustelids

d Track up to 6 centimetres (2 inches) long but rather indistinct, showing 4 small claw marks ➤ rabbits & hares

e Tracks small, hind foot longer than fore, toes with obvious claws. Fore foot may show 4 or 5 toes, hind foot shows 5 toes ➤ rodents & insectivores

Rabbits and hares The soles of the feet of rabbits and hares are covered with a thick layer of forward-pointing hairs which conceal the palmer pads. The four toe pads are also hair-covered so that on firm ground only the claws will leave a mark. On soft ground the position of the feet in the trail is a distinctive feature for these animals, the long hind feet placed side by side behind two circular depressions from the smaller fore feet in a sitting animal, the groups of four tracks showing the hopping or leaping gait as the animal moves (hind in front of fore).

Insectivores and rodents This group of animals really gets the mammal detective guessing since there is such a great overlap in size and appearance in the tracks left by the different species. Those at the extreme ends of the sizes possible may be able to be identified, but others need confirmation of the identity from the finding of droppings, nests or feeding remains. Compare the illustrations (actual size) on p. 88.

All show a similar looking hind foot track with 5 distinct toes and claws, but the insectivores (hedgehog, mole and shrews) show a fore foot with 5 toes, whereas the rodents only show 4 toes on the fore foot. The smaller mammals are very lightweight and only leave discernible tracks in very fine silt or very soft snow.

Watch out for domestic animals and pets that may easily leave trails; some seem to go out of their way to get themselves in print.

The unmistakeable footprints and taildrag (with line of droppings) of a Peak District wallaby in the snow.

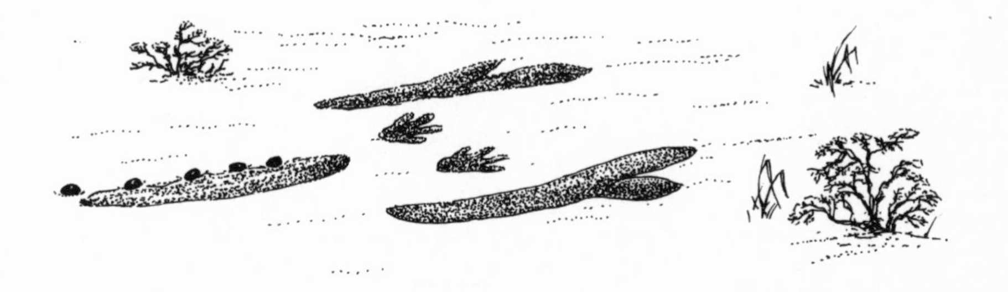

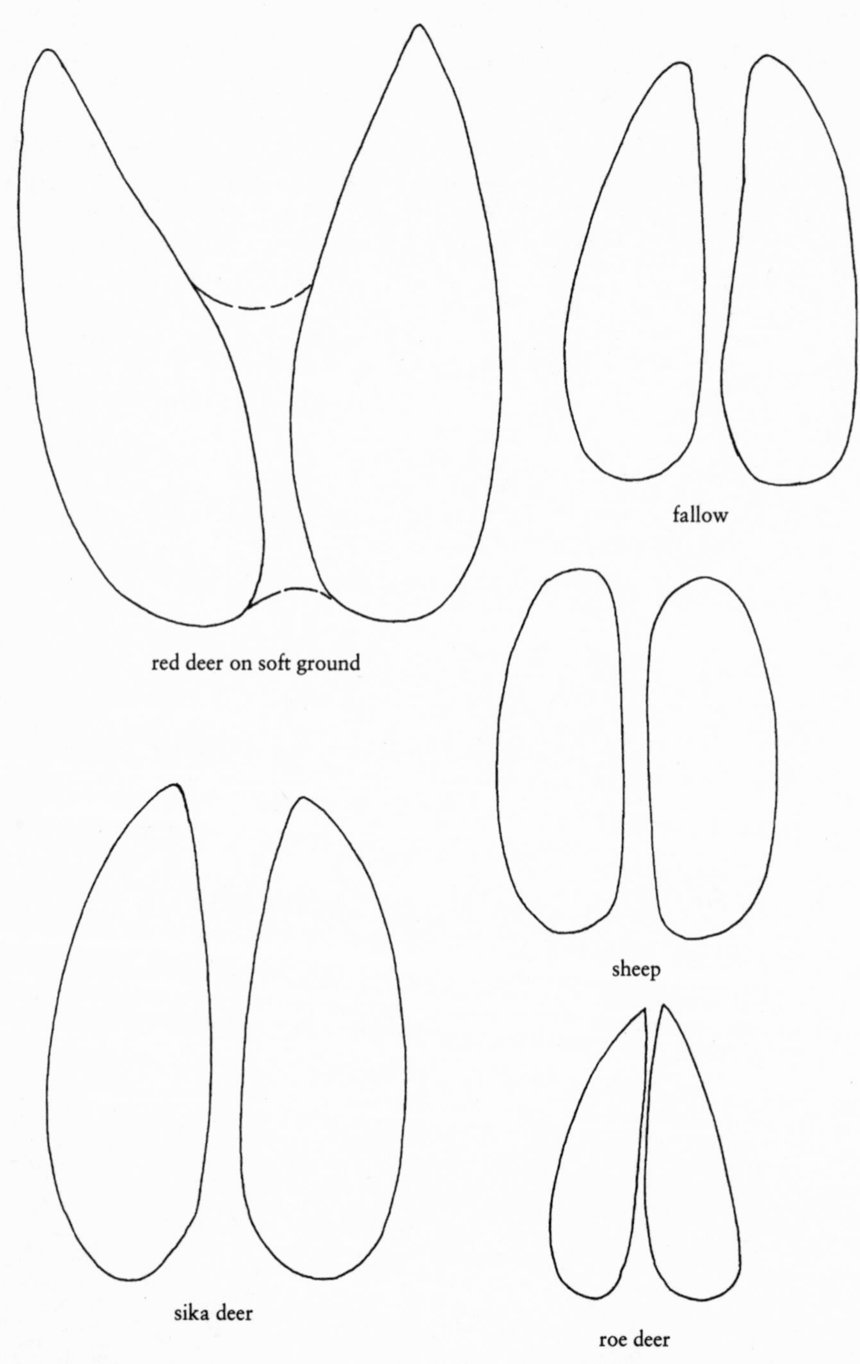

Tracks of mammals with hooves (actual size).

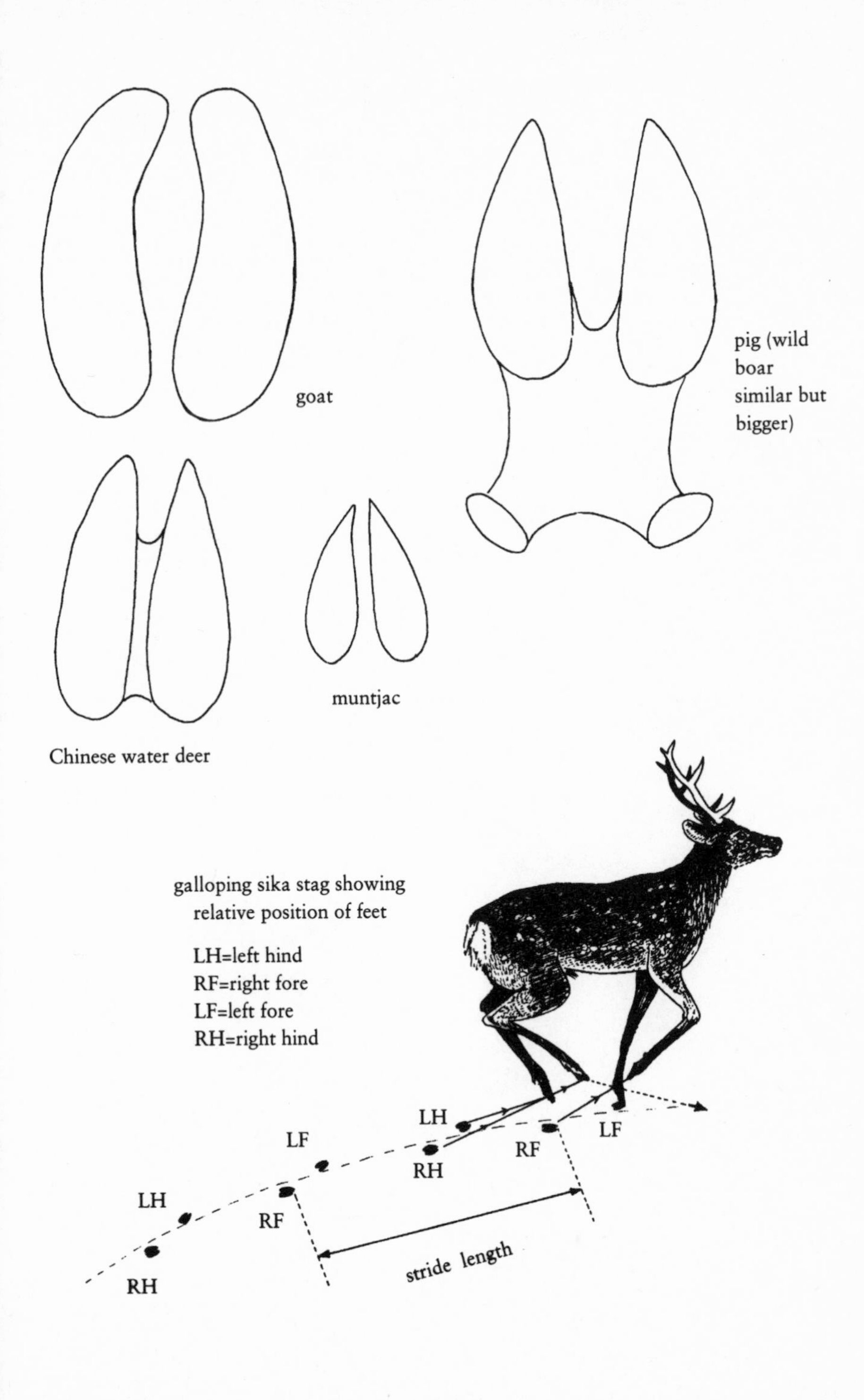
goat
pig (wild
boar
similar but
bigger)
Chinese water deer
muntjac
galloping sika stag showing
relative position of feet
LH=left hind
RF=right fore
LF=left fore
RH=right hind
LH
LF
RF
RH
LF
RF
LH
RF
RH
stride length

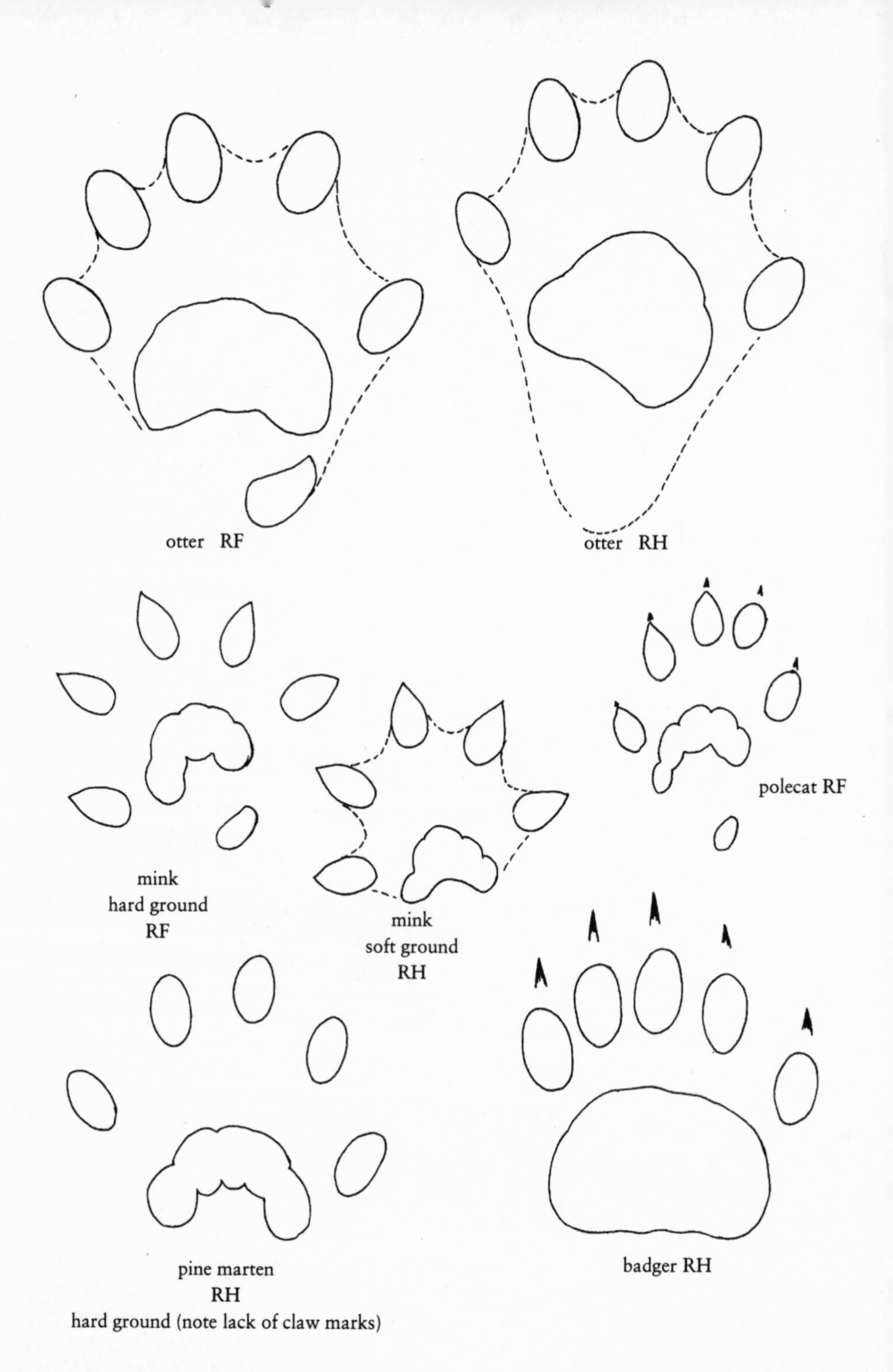
otter RF
otter RH
polecat RF
mink
hard ground
RF
mink
soft ground
RH
pine marten
RH
hard ground (note lack of claw marks)
badger RH

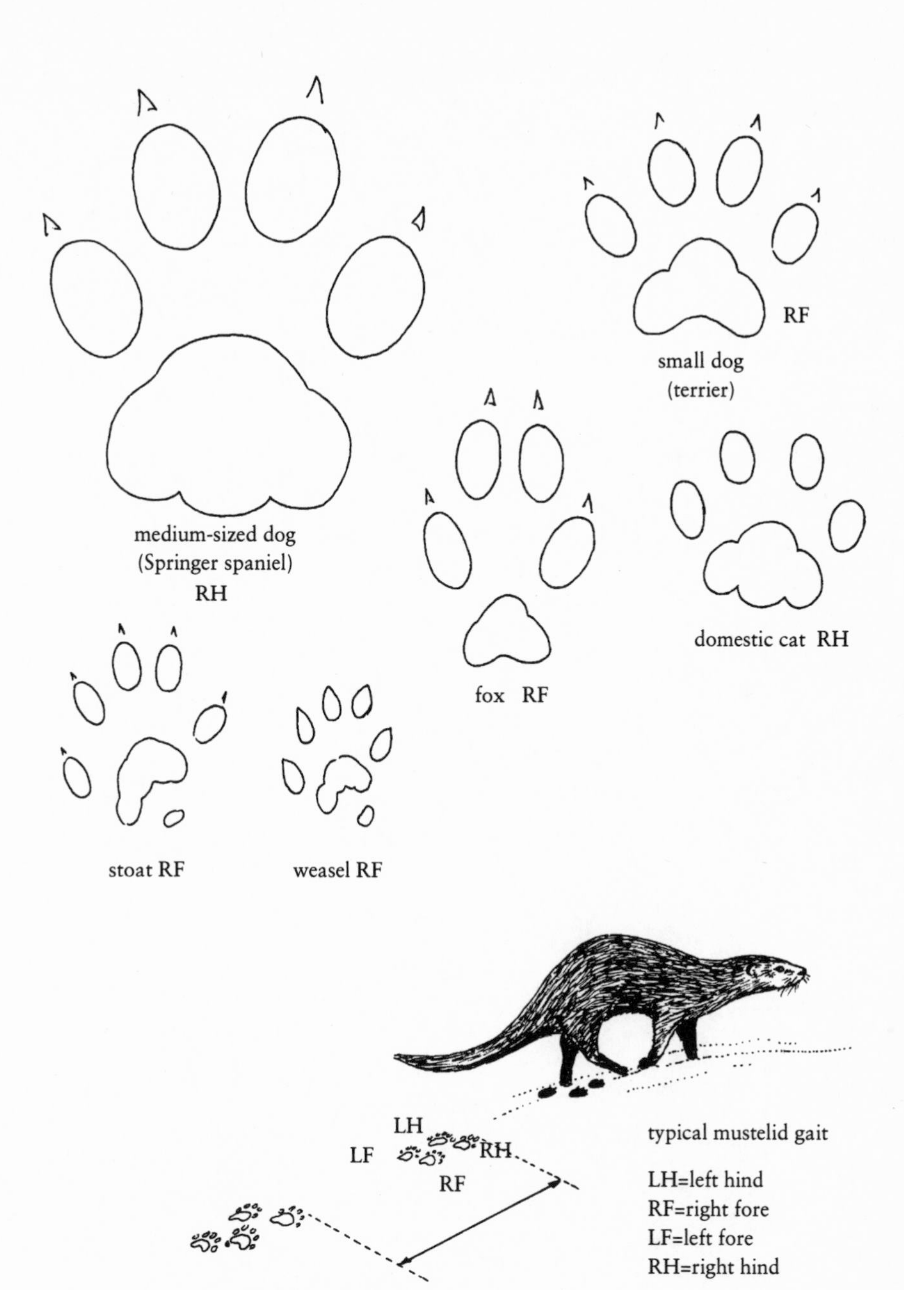

Tracks of mammals with paws (actual size).

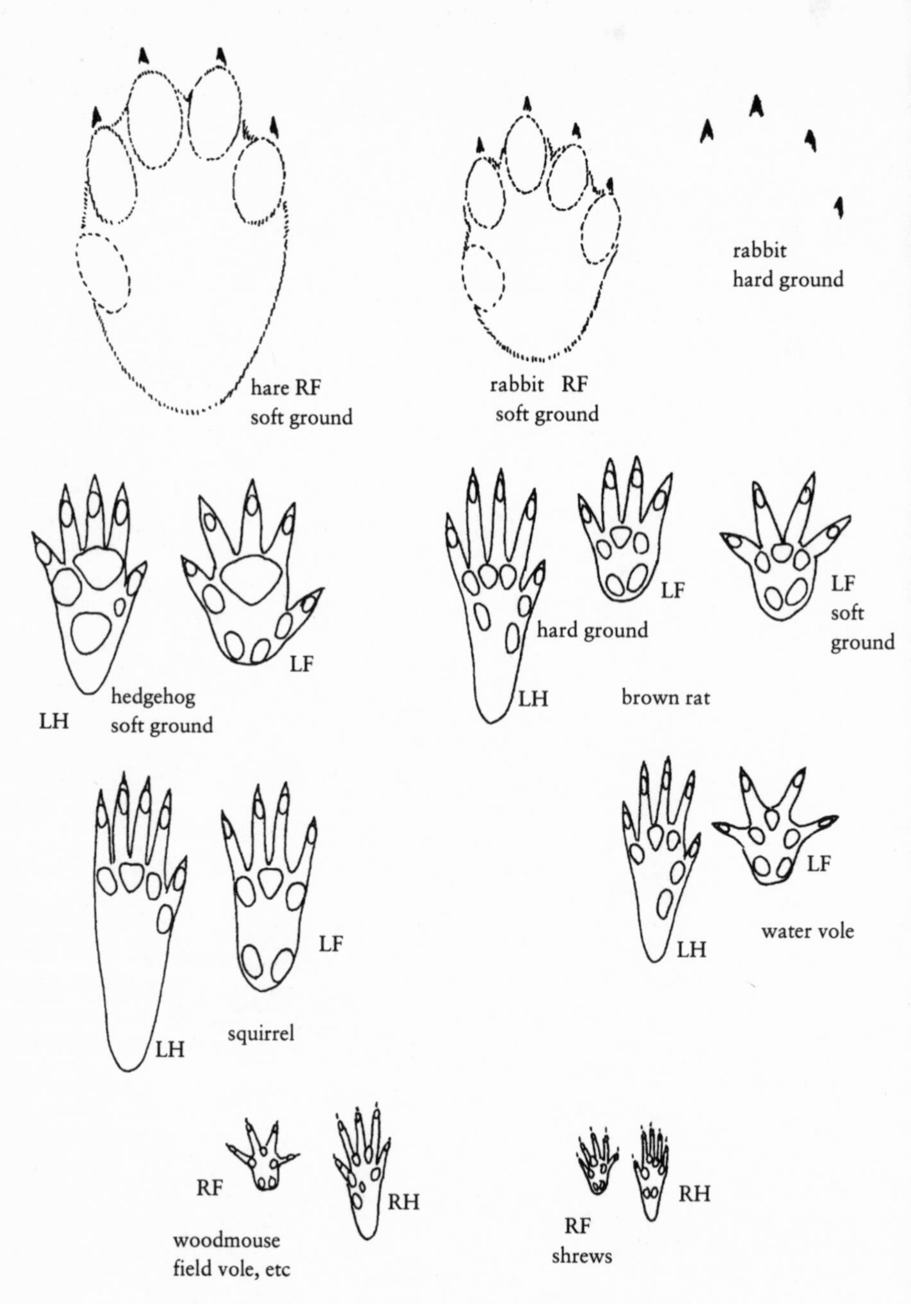

Tracks of rabbits, rodents and insectivores (actual size).

A nose for droppings and odours

The good mammal detective must make use of his or her sense of smell as well as using eyes and ears. Although this sense in people is poorly developed compared to that of a dog, it is still possible to detect the passing of a fox, the spray of a cat or the recently occupied holt of an otter just by scent. Scent plays a very important role in the communication between mammals: it identifies individuals and also indicates whether an animal is in rut or ready to mate. In some species the scent and droppings help mark out the individual's or group's territory. This applies equally to the otter or water vole as a clan of badgers. Other species drop their faeces at random and these play no role in marking territory or in communication, such as the various bats (although the bat colony may use scent to locate and maintain roost sites).

The droppings of mammals carry a scent distinctive of the species but there is some variation depending on what the animal has been eating, whether vegetable, fruit, insects, meat or carrion. Even when two different species have been eating the same food it may be possible to tell the droppings apart by smell although they look identical. Thus a crayfish 'spraint' of an otter smells sweet whereas a crayfish 'scat' of a mink smells disgusting and foul. The characteristic 'ottery' scent had always been difficult for me to describe until one day I was at a friend's house and was offered a selection of speciality teas. By chance I plumped for a cup of jasmine tea and was completely knocked back as the scent of 'essence of otter' hit me from the newly opened packet. It completely put me off drinking it!

The odours from the droppings of deer, rodents and bats are fairly short-lived and it is almost impossible to attempt to describe the subtleties and nuances between the different species. I have hinted at what some of these odours smell like to my nose in the annotated illustrations but they may smell different to you!

Droppings vary in shape and form, size, colour and brightness, consistency and composition, depending on diet and age of the dropping (young animals also may produce smaller droppings than adults). Each species shows some characteristics that help in identification (see drawings). Care should be taken when handling droppings as serious illnesses may be contracted. The safest way is to use a small plastic bag as a glove then turn it inside out to surround the dropping.

As a rule the droppings of herbivores are commonly encountered as groups of spherical or cylindical rounded pellets (herbivores by nature eat large quantities of vegetation and so produce large quantities of droppings). The droppings of carnivores on the other hand occur individually and tend to be longer and sausage-shaped, perhaps twisted with a point at one end (the carnivore produces fewer droppings than the herbivore due to the nutritional value of its diet). Insectivorous animals such as shrews and bats produce pellet-style droppings, whereas hedgehogs produce slender sausage-style ones but in both cases the droppings are fragile and readily crumble to a fine dust with shiny insect fragments.

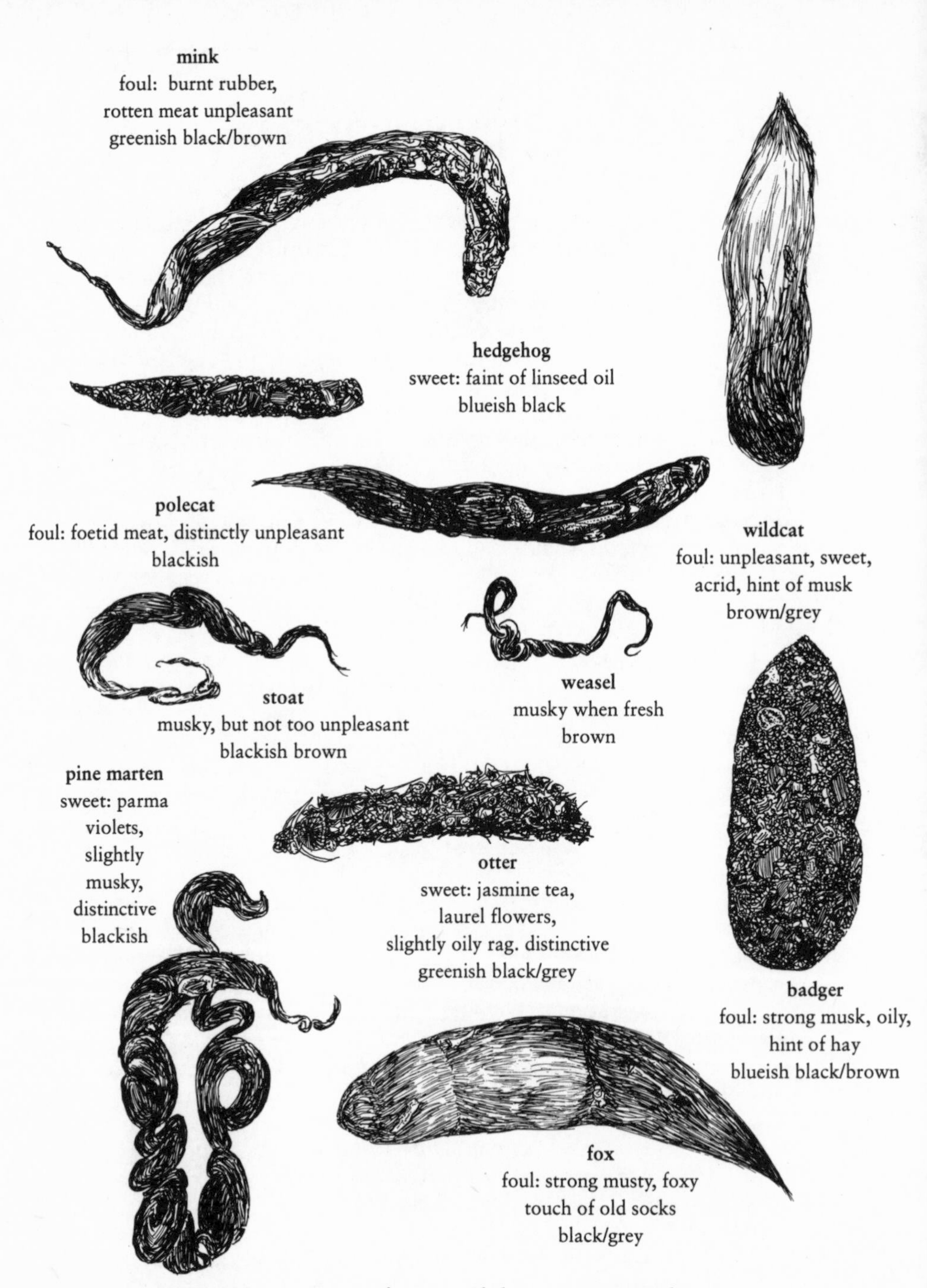

Various types of mammal droppings (actual size).

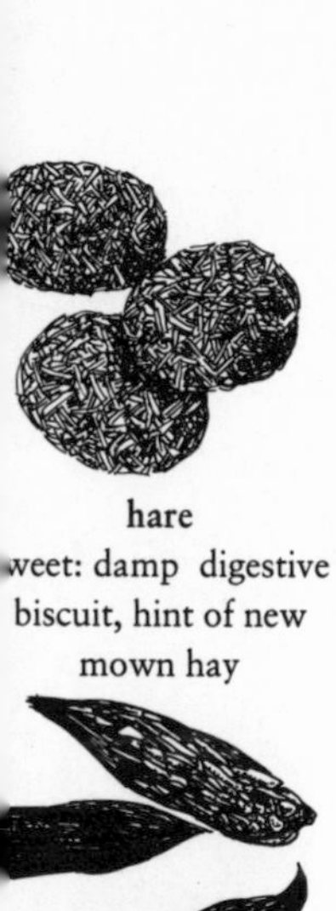

hare
sweet: damp digestive biscuit, hint of new mown hay
greenish brown

rabbit
sweet: damp digestive biscuit, hint ofnew mown hay
yellowish brown/green

red deer
strong, musky
black/brown

rat
foul: rancid food
blackish

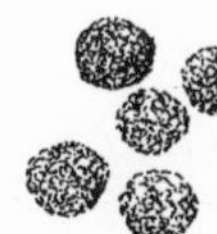

squirrel
sweet: hint of pine sawdust
yellowish

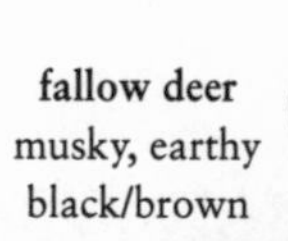

fallow deer
musky, earthy
black/brown

roe deer
earthy, wet leaf litter
blackish

sheep
damp hay
black/brown

water vole
odourless!
brown/green/purple

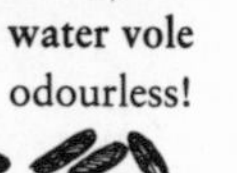

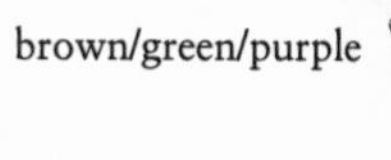

field vole
odourless!
brown/green

goat
strong: musky
black/brown

muntjac
damp hay
black/brown

woodmouse
mousy, damp newspaper
black/brown

house mouse
'mousy' hint of ammonia
blackish

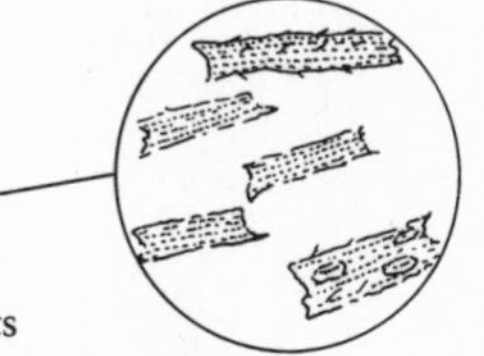

mouse plant fragments

long-eared bat
light brown
hard to crumble

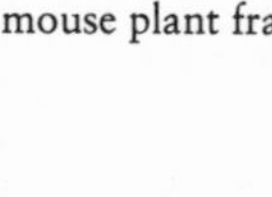

lesser horseshoe
shiny black

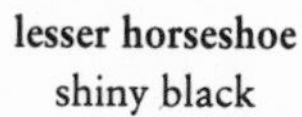

serotine
bat droppings are fairly odour free, except when wet when they smell strongly of ammonia
shiny black

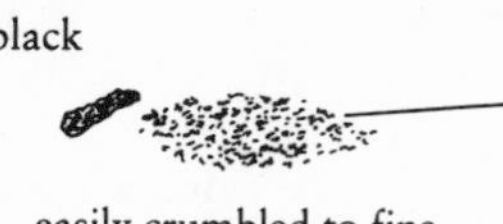

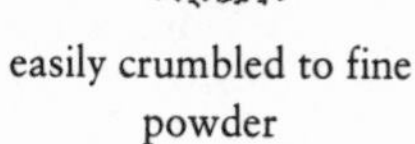

easily crumbled to fine powder

bat insect fragments

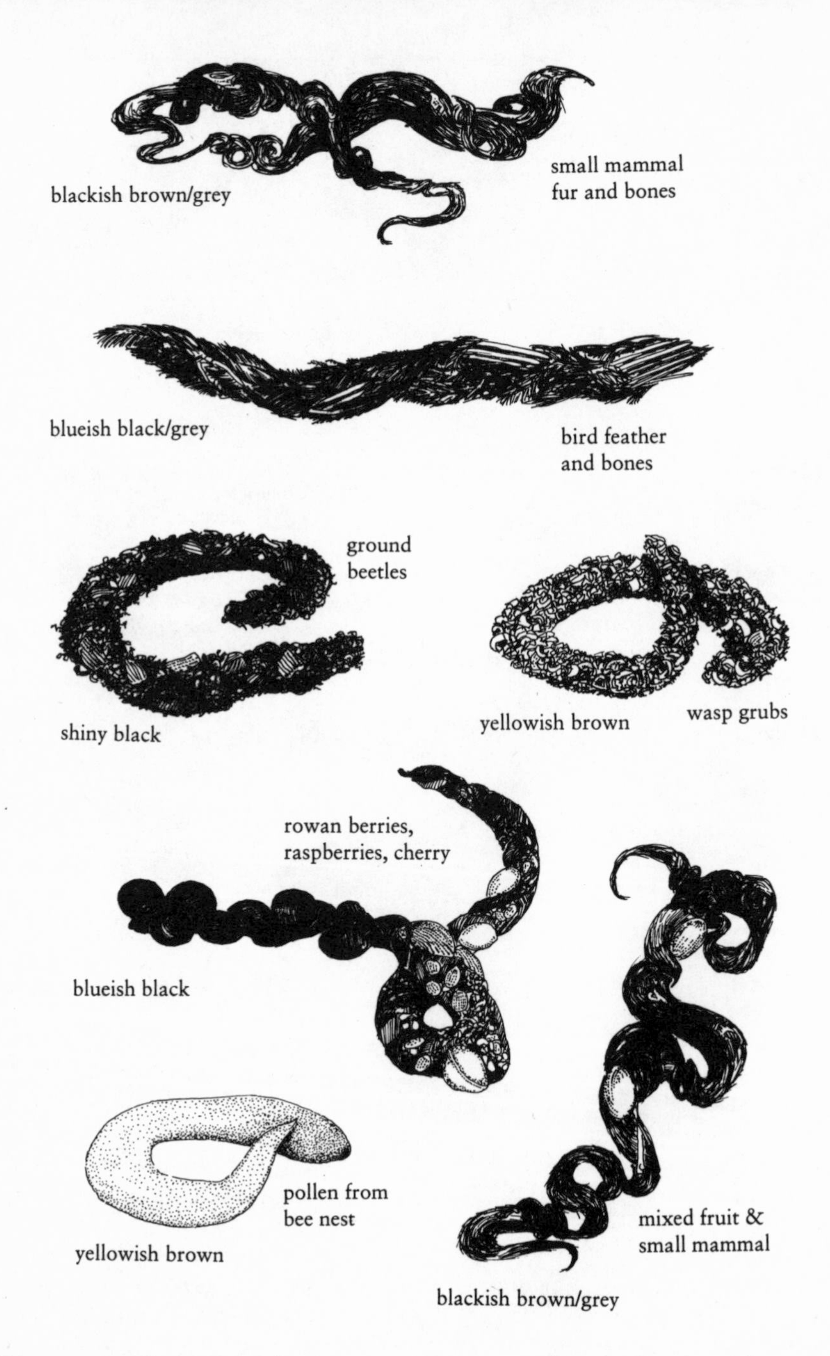

Pine marten droppings, showing variations according to diet (actual size).

Hideaways and places of shelter

A guide to nests, dens, burrows and forms

The mammal detective's power of observation will eventually allow the animal's trail to be followed to its hideout or place of refuge. This is perhaps best searched for during the breeding season when such a site is in constant use for raising young and the adults may be making regular trips back and forth leaving well trodden paths.

The majority of mammals regularly move their sleeping quarters, but all tend to create a permanent home for that time when they have dependant young that need the security of warmth and protection. Many of these sites are hidden from view, perhaps underground in a chamber of a burrow or in a tree hollow. A few species construct aerial nests, like birds, and these are a good indicator of the presence of these mammals. Such specialist nest-builders include the squirrels, dormouse and harvest mouse and these can be identified by their location and size. Woven summer nests are also occasionally made by the field vole and water vole but these are nearly always found close to the ground in the bases of sedges or grass tussocks.

Of the species that build subterranean nests, a number excavate their own burrow systems. Check first to see if there is any freshly dug soil or tracks at the entrance that may tell if the hole is occupied; if cobwebs or fallen sticks lie across the mouth then it is likely to be disused. The size of the hole helps identify who made it.

Choose from the following

a **Small.** Tunnel entrance not more than 3 centimetres (1 inch) diameter, dug by small mammals.

b **Medium.** Tunnel entrance 4-8 centimetres (1.5-3 inches) across, dug by mole, water vole or rat.

c **Large.** Burrow entrance 10-30 centimetres (4-12 inches) across, dug by rabbit, fox or badger. Remember to check the entrance for other field signs such as odour, droppings, tracks or hair tufts to help confirm the occupant of the hole, for many burrows may be taken over by other species. For instance a weasel may appropriate a woodmouse or bank vole hole and a stoat take over a water vole or rat hole. A rabbit burrow may be occupied by stoat, mink, polecat or marten, while a disused badger sett or fox earth may be 'borrowed' by an otter, pine marten or even a wildcat.

The identity of the small mammal that has made the small hole is always difficult to establish and is perhaps best confirmed by 'Longworth trapping' outside. Shrews, voles and mice also burrow under rocks, tree stumps and discarded corrugated metal sheeting.

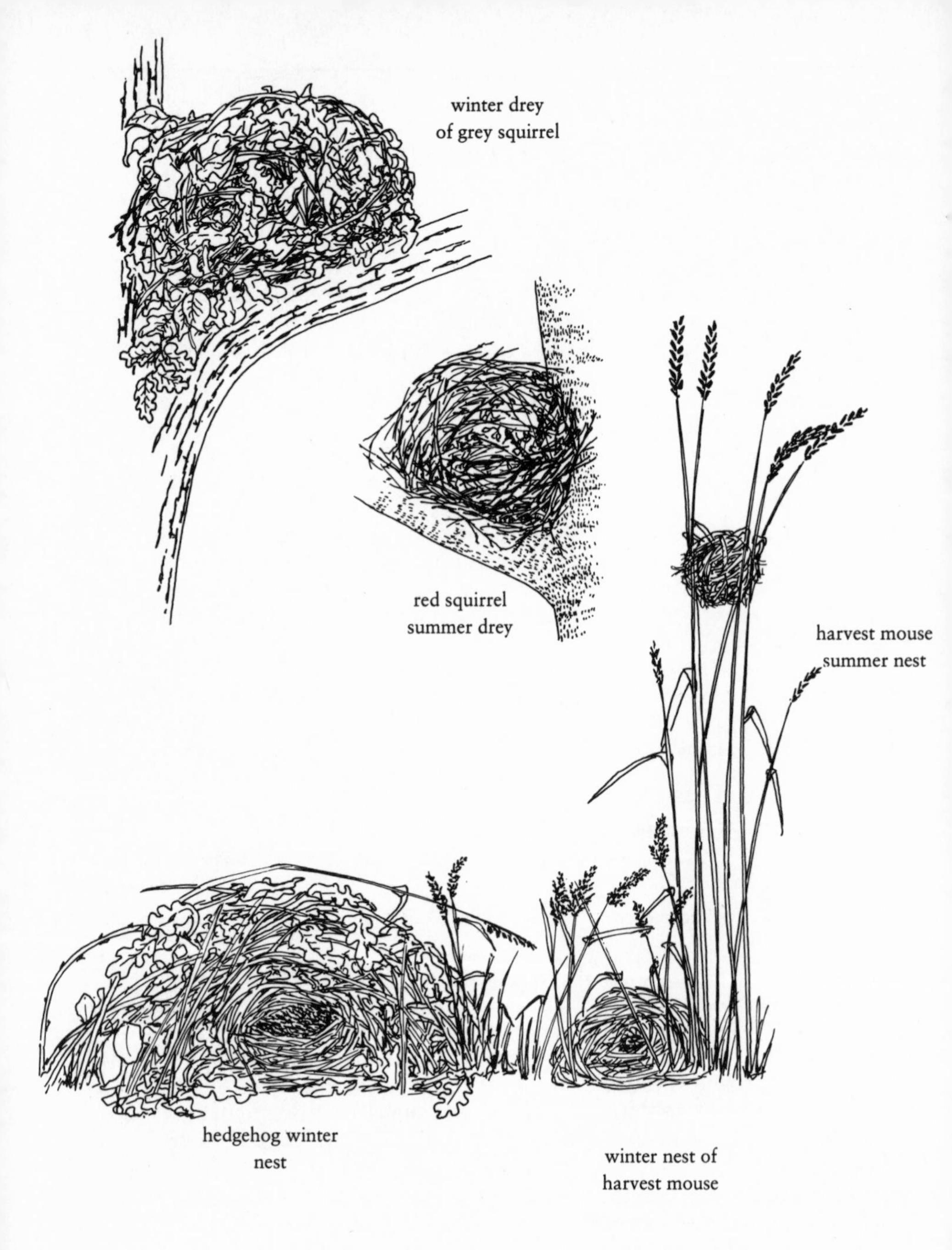

The products of the nest builders.

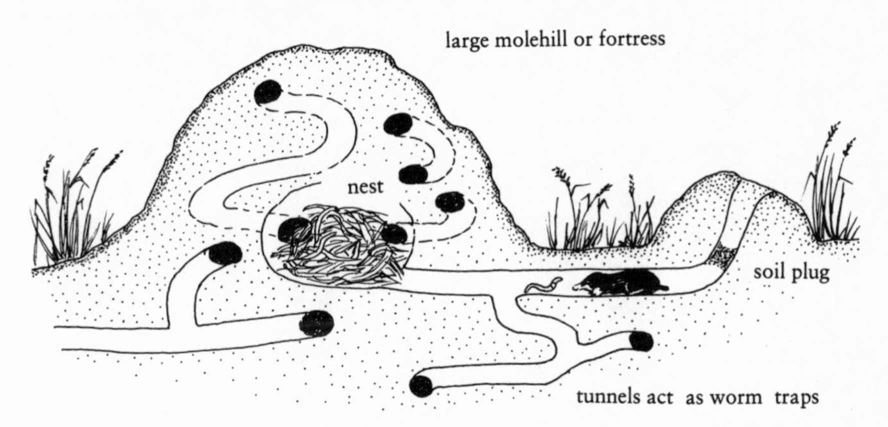

Cross-section through a large mole fortress and a normal molehill.

The mole makes its presence known by its molehills, spoil heaps from its network of burrows. However, occasionally a hole dug by a mole can be found which is slightly oval in cross section (5 centimetres/2 inches broad by 4 centimetres/ 1.5 inches high). Water voles can also dig mole-like tunnels but they do not create the spoil heaps. Normally their multiple entranced burrow system occurs along a watercourse and the holes lie within 3 metres (10 feet) of the bank. Many holes are at the water's edge and some are even below water. Their uppermost holes on the bank are roughly circular (5-7 centimetres/2-3 inches) and show a closely cropped 'lawn' within a 15 centimetre(6 inch) radius of the hole.

Similar to the water vole's holes are those of the brown rat, which are found along watercourses or in field boundaries, but these can be distinguished by a large fan-shaped spoil heap outside and the holes being linked by well trodden runs.

Rabbits live together in large warrens that have many interconnecting burrows. The individual holes are between 8-14 centimetres(3-5.5 inches) in diameter. A series of well trodden runs fan out from the holes.

Another conspicuous hole that may show freshly excavated spoil when occupied is made by the fox. These earths smell strongly of 'fox' and when the fox cubs are old enough to venture out the mammal detective will notice the telltale signs as flattened vegetation littered with chewed sticks, bones, feathers and other 'toys' that they have played with.

Badger holes are easy to recognize, showing a classic low dome shape, broader than high (20-30 centimetres/8-12 inches across); they are often associated with extensive mounds of excavated spoil. Large setts can show up to a dozen or more holes forming terraces of spoil. The spoil is often littered with hay that the badgers have used for bedding.

Natural cavities that occur in tree hollows, under tree roots, in log piles and

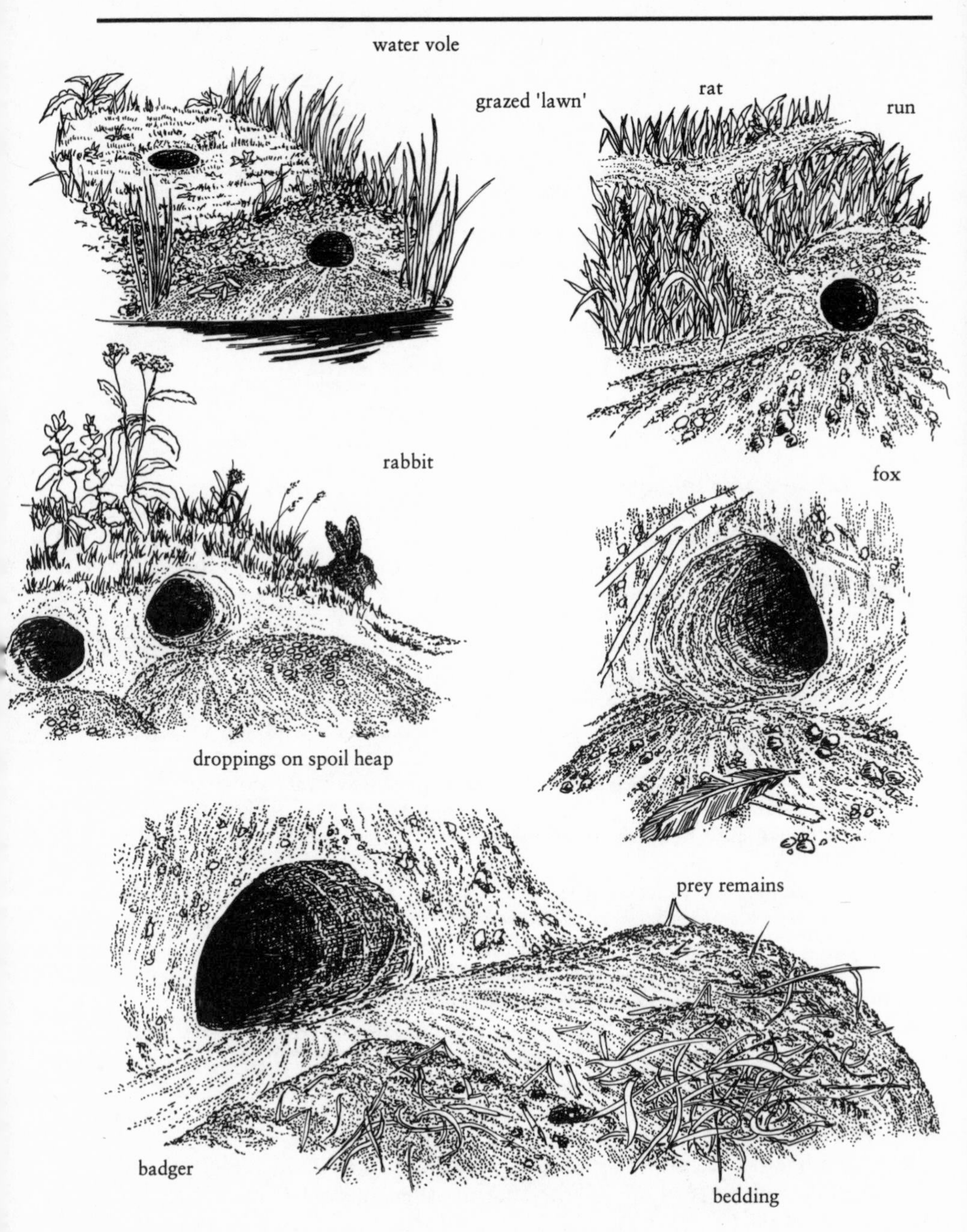

Relative shapes and sizes of burrows made by larger mammals.

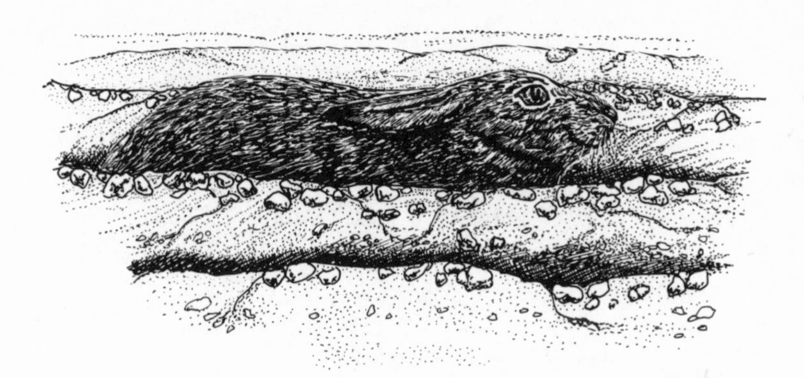

The form of the brown hare is little more than a scrape.

among rock screes are used by many species including those that would normally dig their own burrows.

Old willow pollards lining the banks of our low lying rivers make particularly good den sites for both otter and mink but I was amazed to find the hollows of one old pollard being used by 20 or so rabbits. One even had a lookout post 3 metres above the ground.

Disused woodpecker holes and larger natural holes higher up a tree trunk may be used by bats, dormice, squirrels or pine martens.

Some mammals never use a specific place of shelter but simply rest on the ground. Forms are shallow scrapes or flattened vegetation on the ground that are

The otter couch can often be found in the open among tall grasses, sedges and reeds.

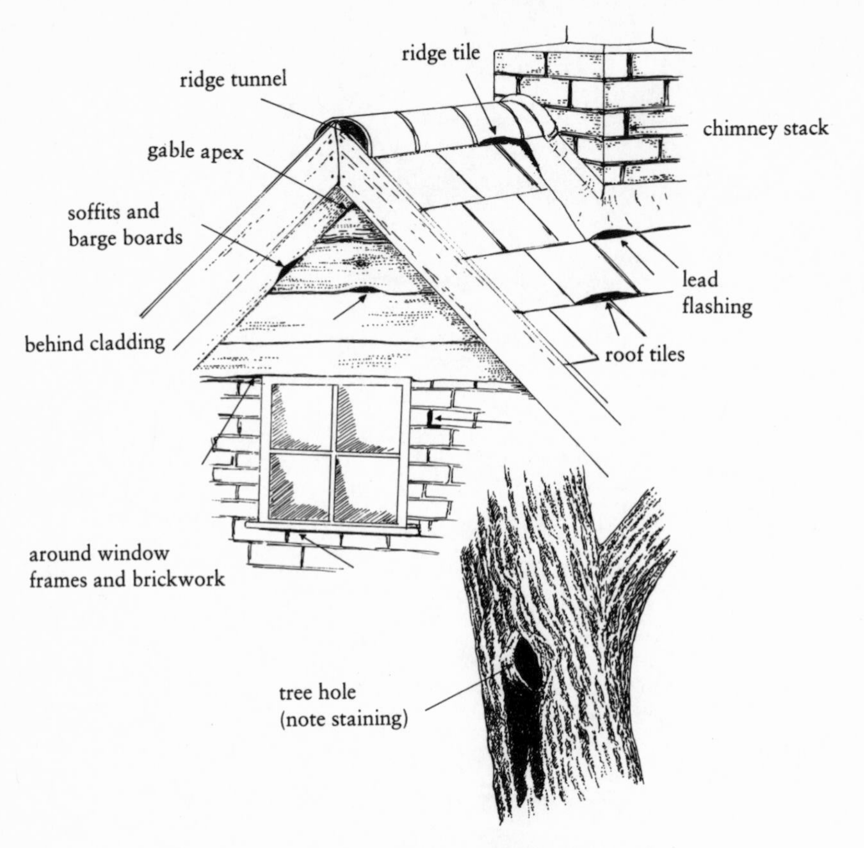

The various nooks and crannies used by bats.

made by deer and hares, which when in brambles or beside grass tussocks may conceal the animal very well. You may gain some clues as to which species had laid there by the size of the form and the droppings nearby.

Fox, wildcat and otter may also lie up above ground in shrubbery, reeds or grass tussocks forming 'couches' like those of deer.

Field boundaries are good places to look for mammal burrows and other shelters particularly if the hedge bottom is densely vegetated (a good place to look for hedgehogs). Dry stone walls may offer suitable den sites for stoats and weasels.

Outbuildings around farms and houses may provide further hideaways for small mammals, rats, polecats, hedgehogs and urban foxes as well as roost sites for bats. Some species of bat have been quick to adapt to man-made structures and will occupy crevices in bridges, churches and dwelling houses (in loft spaces, under roof tiles, in wall cavities and behind external cladding).

Feeding remains and other field signs

The detective on the trail of a particular mammal will soon find traces where the animal has stopped to feed, especially if the mammal in question is a herbivore – a nibbled twig here, a grazed stem there and so on. Carnivores, however, may need to be tracked over long distances before evidence of a kill is found.

Always examine an animal's feeding place, since this can reveal a great deal about its habits and diet.

Grazers and browsers A sure way to tell if shoots have been bitten off by deer rather than by rabbits, hares or rodents is to examine the shoot end for fraying. This is because deer (as well as goats and sheep) have lower incisors but lack upper ones (they are replaced by a horny plate in the roof of the mouth). The chisel-like teeth of rabbits, hares and rodents leave clean cut, oblique bite marks. The effect on the growth of young trees can also indicate the presence of the various browsers: the removal of the top shoot causing the tree to send out more side branches, sometimes forming a distinct basal 'frill', is particularly noticeable among young conifer plantations that harbour roe deer.

Shoots of herbaceous plants and grasses that show browsing or grazing are very difficult to pin down to a particular species with any degree of certainty and the mammal detective will often have to find other clues such as footprints or droppings to help prove the culprit's identity. The signs of grazing are usually the

*Bitten shoots (*left*) and winter barking (*right*) signs.*

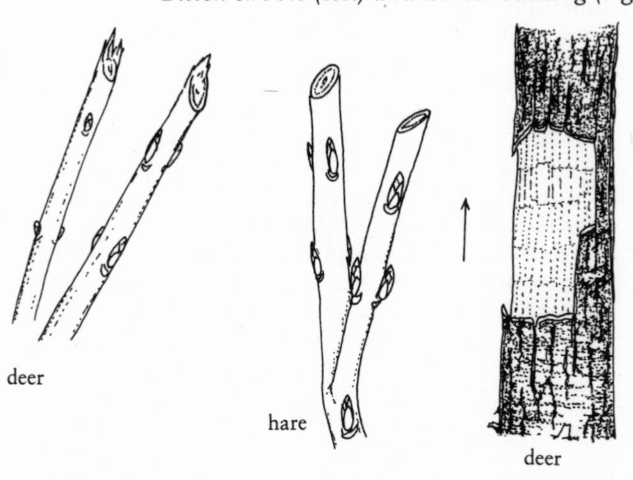

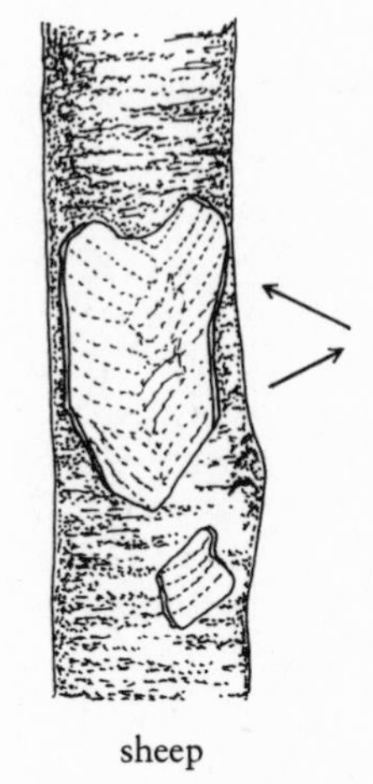

Barking on young apple tree (left) *by hare and field vole. Note the deep bites of the hare, leaving furrows. The ground level barking of the field vole can form a complete ring that will kill the tree.* (Right) *Barking on young fir tree by bank vole. Note this climbing vole has gnawed the branches where they join the trunk.*

close cropping of plants to ground level and this can be very obvious in some arable fields, such as winter sown cereals. Remember that rabbits maintain the short turf of chalk downland and coastal cliff tops.

Many browsers also eat bark and the signs can be distinctive and long lasting, often several months after the event. Deer use their lower incisors like planes and gouge a series of grooves along the surface when the bark is firmly attached during the winter months. Summer barking takes place when the bark is loose and can be pulled off in long shreds. The size of the teeth marks and the position and extent of the damage help identify which species was probably responsible (see below).

Gnawers and nibblers On woody plants the most obvious feeding signs are gnawed bark or roots and this is most frequently found during the winter months.

Gnawed and frayed bark high in the branches is most likely to have been carried out by squirrels or occasionally smaller climbing rodents. Barking at ground level, especially on young trees, is frequently done by voles and can sometimes be severe enough to kill the tree (if the bark has been removed all round the tree – known as ring barking). The gnawed bark shows the marks of both upper and lower incisors on the surface of the wood as broad or fine streaks, depending on the species involved.

A guide to incisor gnaw marks

Width of incisors (across all the teeth)	*Species responsible*
< 2.5mm	bank vole, field vole, woodmice
3.5 – 4.5mm	water vole, brown rat
6.0 – 10.0mm	rabbit, hare
10.0 – 30.0mm	muntjac, roe, fallow, red deer

Root gnawing is also carried out, more frequently in winter, by ground dwelling rodents, but it is not as obvious unless the tree dies, topples over or is dug up.

The various vole species spend most of the summer eating herbaceous plants and grasses, the stems of which they gnaw through, then take to a nearby feeding station and cut up into preferred lengths that can be easily held in the front paws. The length of the cut stems (c.10 centimetres/4 inches) and the size of the teeth marks help identify the water vole from the other species (droppings would confirm this).

At certain times of the year the **dormouse** specializes in nibbling flowers, taking the nutritious nectaries and anthers. The discarded remains of honeysuckle flowers that show their nectaries bitten out may confirm the presence of this elusive mammal.

Signs on cones, seeds and fruits One very obvious piece of evidence of gnawing mammals in conifer forests is the discarded cone. This can be one of the best ways of detecting the presence of squirrels, which handle the cones differently from rats, mice and voles.

Since the animals are after the nutritious seeds, the scales have to be bitten off first (as opposed to being prised apart by the beaks of birds such as the crossbill). Depending on whether the squirrel or woodmouse has held the cone's top end to the right or to the left while gnawing, the bitten scale will show an oblique cut one way or the other. Since each individual animal always handles the cones exactly

The different ways mice (and dormice) and voles open hazelnuts.

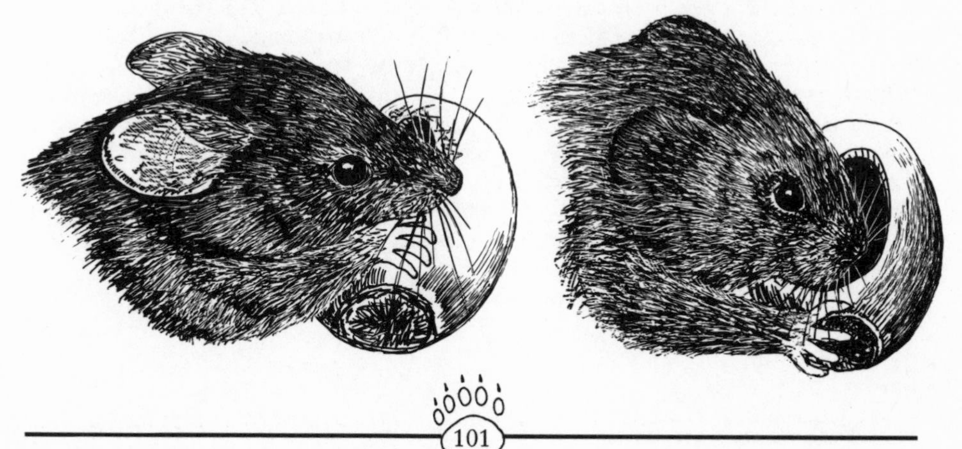

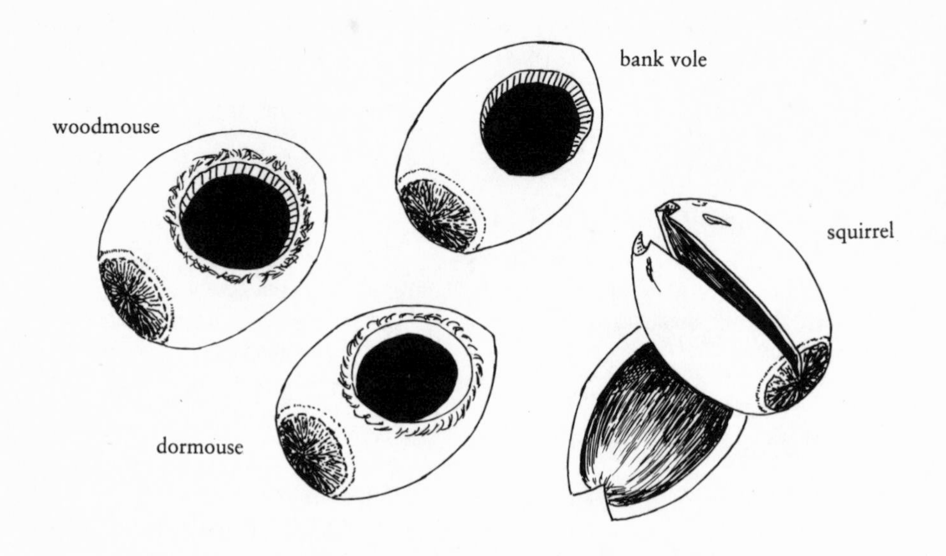

The nibbled nut: note scratch marks around hole and chiselled face of hole edge in woodmouse; unscratched surface and chiselled edge in bank vole; scratched surface but smooth gouged out inner edge in dormouse; nut prized apart through notch in top of shell in squirrel.

the same way each time, they can be divided into left-handed or right-handed operators. Cones stripped by mice and voles are not so readily found as 'squirrel cones' because they prefer to take them into cover, out of sight from potential predators. Once located, however, these secure feeding stations can often show large accumulations of cones.

The nibbled nut Hazelnuts are favoured by many rodents and the identification of the tooth marks requires an understanding of how the nut was handled. With squirrels the animal first makes a little notch in the top of the nut, then the lower incisors are used like a crowbar to split the shell in two. Woodmice, yellow-necked mice and hazel dormice hold the nut against the ground or branch and, once a hole is made, gnaw at the side furthest away from the body as they turn the nut. This action marks the outside of the nut with the upper incisors (see illustrations). The voles, however, once they have made a hole, insert their noses and gnaw at the nearest side, without marking the outside of the nut.

Not all mice and voles know what to do with a hazelnut, however, for in order to make these observations a friend of mine caught a number of bank voles, field voles and woodmice and kept them captive while he fed them different nuts and fruit. Only those mice and voles that came from hedgerows with hazel opened the nuts straight away. The small mammals from fields with no hazel growing nearby either had difficulty breaking into the nut or failed to recognize it as food.

Acorns, beech mast, rosehips and many fruits may all show the gnawings of rodents.

Nibbled snails Although most rodents are strictly vegetarian, they will occasionally supplement their diet with invertebrates. Rats, water voles and woodmice,

Nibbled cones.

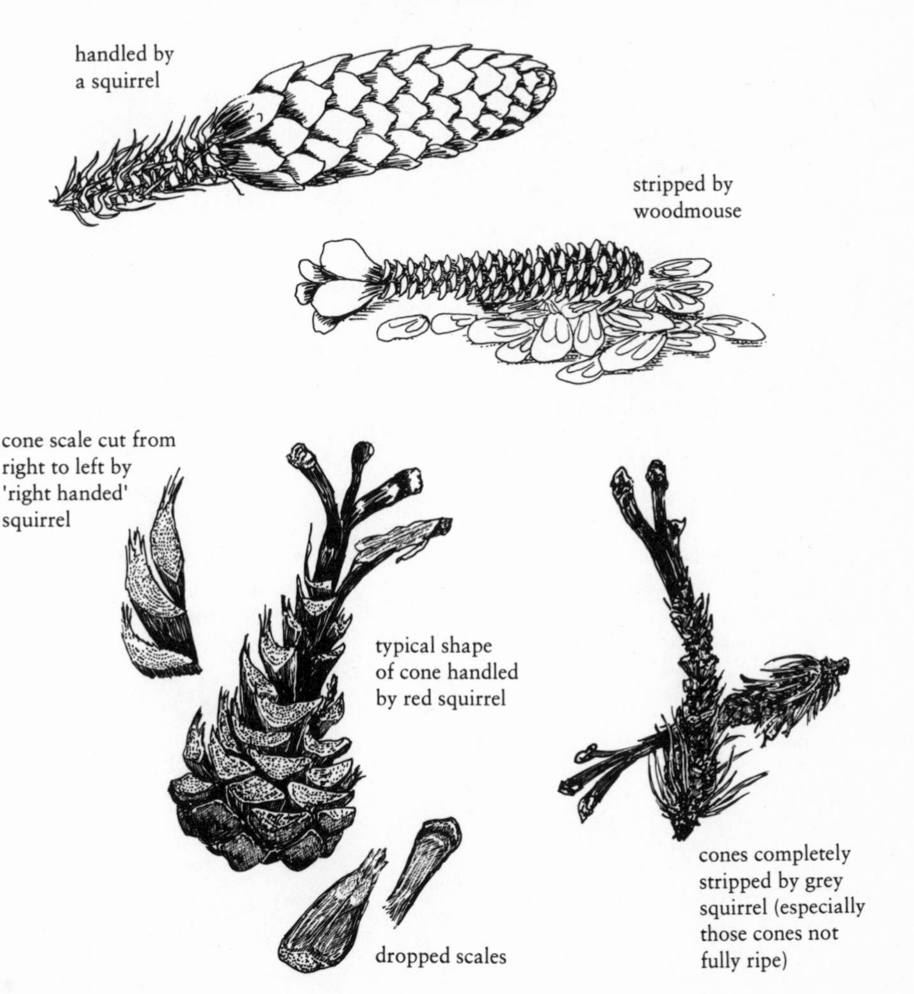

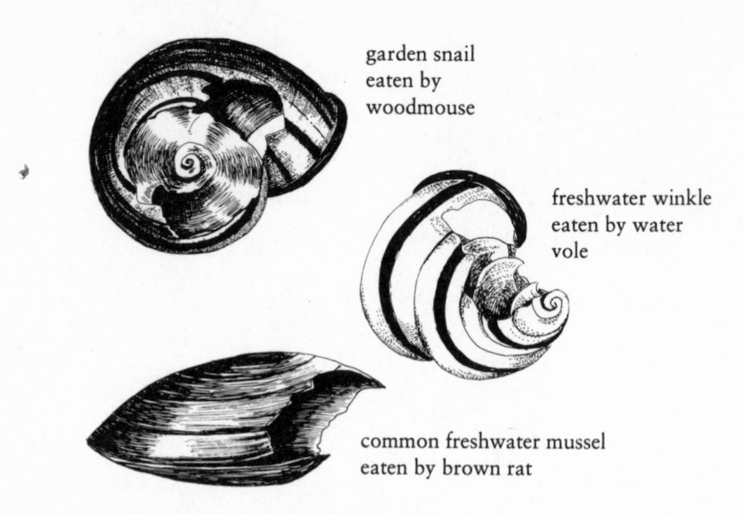

Nibbled snails.

from time to time, take snails (and in the case of the former two, river mussels as well). The bite marks are clearly seen concentrated on the spire of the shell (song thrushes smash the shell open on a rock). Accumulations of snail shells can be found hidden under grass tussocks beside the animal's run.

Feeding signs left by predators The remains left by a predator will depend on the size of the prey. Small prey are swallowed whole, while larger prey may leave plenty of remains, giving the detective the chance of identifying the predator. However in practice this can be difficult due to the fact that other animals may have visited to scavenge. At the carcass of a red deer which had died from starvation one winter, I found footprints in the snow of fox, pine marten, stoat, buzzard, crows, gulls and even shrews where they had come to feed.

Where a large animal has been killed by a predator the signs usually show that the belly has been opened first and the liver and lungs eaten before starting on the flesh. Bite marks on the bones will give clues as to the predator's identity since the relative size and distance between the canine marks can help separate fox from badger from mink, etc.

In many cases the prey items are taken back to the predator's place of refuge or hidden feeding place where the carcass or remains may be buried under leaves, soil or snow and returned to later. At the site of the kill, blood and tufts of fur or feathers may be the only sign that anything has happened.

The carnivore's carnassial teeth come into play when the prey is a bird, since the wing and tail feathers will show that they have been sheared off rather than plucked out. The animal's saliva sticks feather tufts together and these are scattered around the carcass (if it has not been carried away). Bird bones show clear

Woodpigeon tail feathers sheared off by a fox.

signs of being bitten or crushed and the back of the head is usually missing.

Surplus killing Foxes and many of the mustelid species seem to go on a 'killing frenzy' when they get amongst a bird nesting colony, into a dovecot or in a hen house. The abundance of prey, the confined space, the ease of killing and the birds' panic probably trigger an overkill response and they will kill many more birds than they want to eat or can drag away.

Other prey items Along a river bank or lake edge the feeding remains of the otter, mink and polecat may be encountered. Remains of fish will depend on their size but often show a scattering of scales, the fish's tail fin and a bitten head. All three mustelids will also take crayfish, frogs and toads and the various canine marks may be found on the remains. Frogs and toads are dealt with by skinning and leaving the head and body turned inside out.

Various mammals will also eat eggs, especially martens, foxes, mink, polecats and hedgehogs, the latter taking clutches of ground nesting birds in situ, the others tending to carry them off individually. Canine puncture holes may help identify

Mink at moorhen's nest.

the culprit. For instance, the distance between holes in the mink, polecat and marten are 14 mm, 16 mm and 20 mm respectively.

Examining jaws and teeth The number of incisors, canines, pre-molars and molars of a particular species make up a code known as the dental formulae, that places it in a particular family and may even allow identification to species level. Three extreme examples are given below:

	common shrew	**pine marten**	**roe deer**
	insectivore	*carnivore*	*herbivore*
upper jaw	3.1.3.3	3.1.4.1.	0.0.3.3.
lower jaw	1.1.1.3.	3.1.4.2.	3.1.3.3.

Incisors These are the chisel-like front teeth that are for cutting. They are most obvious among the rodents, rabbits and hares, continually growing throughout their lives but are worn down by regular gnawing. Misaligned incisors often grow to bizarre lengths. Rabbits and hares also have a smaller extra pair of incisors hidden behind the larger cutting pair and this feature helps distinguish them from large rodents (a hare skull and coypu skull are of similar size).

In deer there are no upper incisors, just a horny plate, but the lower jaw shows

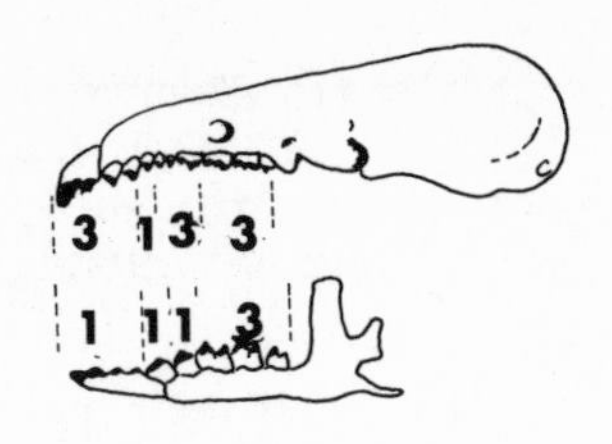

shrew
3 1 3 3
1 1 1 3

pine marten
3 1 4 1
3 1 4 2

roe deer
0 0 3 3
3 0 3 3

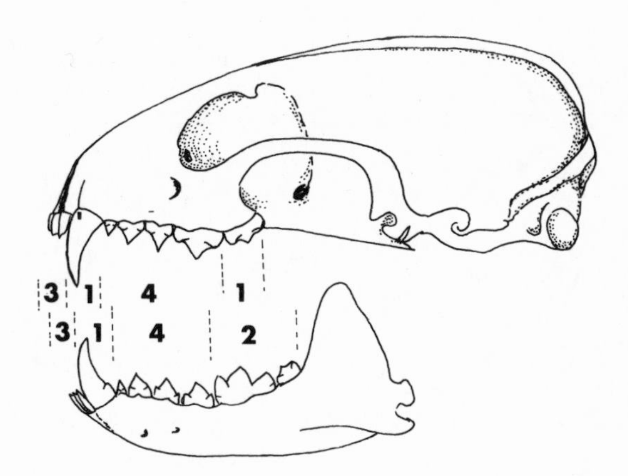

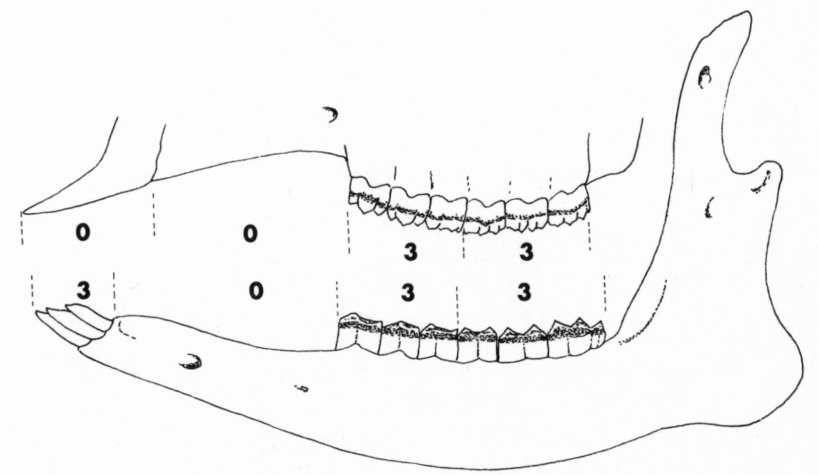

Dental formulae of shrew, pine marten and roe deer.

four pairs of incisors (the fourth is really a modified canine in disguise).

In most bat species the incisors are much reduced in size and almost impossible to see in the live animal. This is because they need to be small to avoid interfering with the ultrasound the bat makes while navigating or hunting.

Canines These are also known as eye teeth and are used for holding, ripping and tearing. They are most obvious as big dagger-like single teeth in the upper and lower jaws of carnivores, especially among the dog, cat and weasel families. Seals, dolphins and toothed whales are supreme fish-eating specialists and their teeth are instantly recognizable as all being canine-like, for dealing with their prey.

In addition to the normal deer teeth, the muntjac and Chinese water deer males develop enlarged upper canines as dagger-like tusks for fighting rivals. Red and sika deer however may develop short rounded upper canines known as tushes. Rodents, rabbits and hares do not have canines but show a pronouned gap between the incisors and cheek teeth known as the diastema.

Cheek teeth – a question of shearing or grinding? The carnivores have specialized shearing cheek teeth, modified premolars and molars known as carnassials. These have given the group their predatory ability of shearing through flesh and bone. For instance in the otter the carnassials are wide and sharp with three crests allowing them to slice through the flesh of fish and crunch up bones or the carapaces of crayfish and crabs.

Among hedgehogs, moles, shrews and bats, the cheek teeth can appear carnassial-like since they are used for crunching through the tough outer coats of insects.

Herbivorous animals need to grind their food down finely for digestion, so the cheek teeth are broad, relatively large with flat or ridged surfaces. These are most obvious among the rodents and deer families. In deer the white enamel becomes worn with age until flat and smooth and less efficient at grinding.

Ageing an animal by its teeth How worn the teeth have become as the animal gets older has long been used to assess the age; for instance, badgers approaching 10 years (or more) will often show teeth that have virtually worn away, being little more than stubs and many may be missing, having fallen out. This is because badgers eat a lot of worms that are packed with gritty mud. Estimating the amount of tooth wear requires a good knowlege of what healthy new permanent teeth should look like, but with practice you can calculate age along the lines of 10 per cent loss for each year of age. This means that the upper incisors of a carnivore such as a fox will be 60 per cent lost by the time they are 6 or 7 years old. A more accurate technique requires the preparation of the tooth for the microscope (so can only be used on dead specimens). The teeth of all mammals are anchored in their sockets by a hard substance called cementum which is strengthened with new layers, year after year. To see the growth lines, the tooth is first soaked in a weak solution of nitric acid to remove the calcium, which leaves the tooth soft and rubbery. Using a machine called an ultra microtome, that cuts very thin sections through the tooth root, a thin slither of tooth is placed on a microscope slide

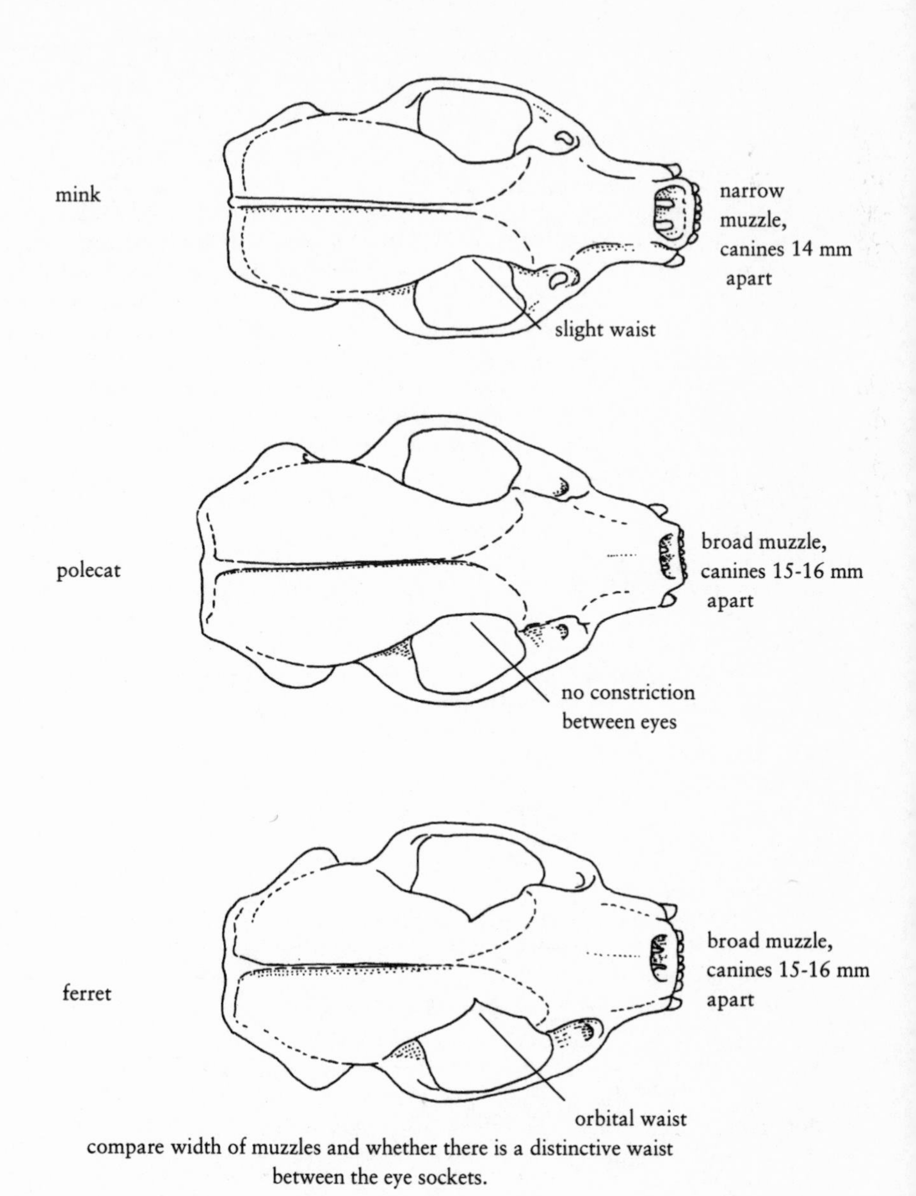

Comparison of three very similar mustelid skulls (actual size).

and stained with a blue dye. The annual growth lines can then be seen and counted under low power magnification in much the same way as counting tree rings. The lines are always formed in the autumn or winter so the date of the animal's death is also required to give the best estimate of age (see illustration).

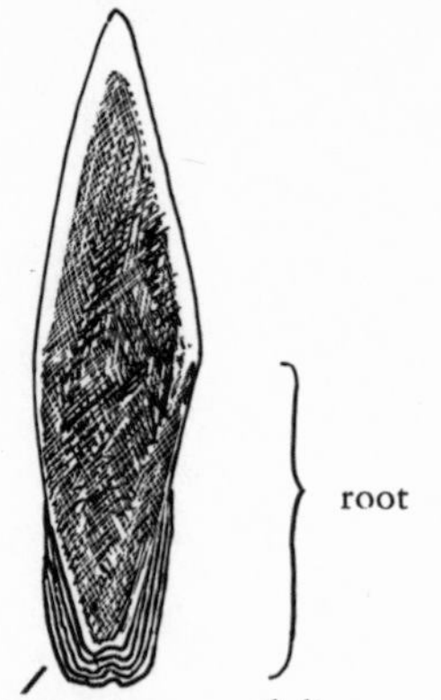

Cross section through a mink canine tooth.

Skulls The position of the eye socket and the length and breadth measurements may give enough clues as to its identity even if no jaw or teeth are present in the skull fragment. Slightly forward-pointing eye sockets, allowing binocular vision, are evident in the predatory species giving them the ability to judge distance. Eyes of prey species on the other hand may be positioned on either side of the head allowing all-round vision for better awareness of potential predators.

The skull also provides the attachment of the jaw muscle: animals with a powerful bite show a ridge of bone along the top of the cranium (sagittal crest). This is one of the most obvious features in the adult badger. In juveniles the sagittal crest is much smaller so the feature can help determine the animal's age.

Skulls of rabbits are seemingly the most frequent bone fragments to be encountered while out for a walk in the British countryside. This perhaps reflects the animal's size and superabundance; also, as a result of myxamotosis, infected rabbits die above ground in large numbers.

Limb bones If the skull and teeth are missing, the next bones useful in identification are the limb bones, shoulder blades and pelvic bones. Their overall length can indicate the animal's size and the shape of the ends (epiphyses) can help assign it to a family if not genera or species. The humerus of the mole is very distinctive (see illustration).

In bats the simple measurement of the forearm length can sometimes correctly identify species. For instance a measurement of more than 47 mm will help separate the Noctule from the Leisler's bat (see pp. 72-4).

Limb bones may also be used to help estimate the age of a specimen. The epiphyses slowly turn to hard bone as the animal reaches its full size. An X-ray of the long bones will show the relative degree of hardening or closure of the epiphyses and this will help estimate a young animal's age. In bats the finger bones show this feature very well among juveniles, just by holding the wing up to the light, the gaps at the joints can be seen.

Humerus of mole.

Bat feeding perches Greater horseshoes, Natterer's and long-eared bats bring larger insects back to a regular feeding perch where the moth wings and beetle wing cases (and other parts)

Moth wings, butterfly wings (taken while roosting) and droppings below a long-eared bat feeding perch in a farm shed.

may be dropped. The bat droppings help identify the species of bat, and the insect wings that accumulate can be identified by the mammal detective to give information about the bats' diet. Try looking in your local church porch for these signs.

Snuffle holes and dug-out nests Badgers feeding on worms, grubs and plant roots produce characteristic snuffle holes that are easily identified by the mammal detective (they can cause a lot of damage to lawns, bowling greens, golf courses

Signs of deer fraying.

Red deer antler cast on heather moor.

and cricket pitches so you may get called in to investigate and come up with solutions such as diverting the most obvious badger path).

Sometimes it's possible to find evidence that the underground nest chamber of rabbits, water voles and small rodents has been dug out and the young eaten by a badger or fox. The detective will recognize the nest as a ball of fine hay on top of the dug soil next to the hole.

Badger, fox and pine marten will sometimes dig out wasp and bee nests to eat the grubs or pollen stores.

Wallows Many deer create shallow pits in swampy places where they can lie and cover themselves in a mud bath. A nearby tree may also be coated in mud where the animal has rubbed itself against it on leaving the wallow. Red deer stags do this during the rut and such wallows take on a very strong odour.

Tree fraying This is easily recognized and is caused by the male deer rubbing the antlers when they are fully formed and the skin that surrounds them (the velvet) has become loose. The shed velvet is then eaten by the deer and so is rarely found. Unlike other deer, the roe buck continues to rub its antlers as a method of marking its territory (it has a scent gland on its forehead).

Cast antlers At the end of the rut the males shed their antlers and start to grow a new, bigger set. These are nearly always found singly and are fairly easy to identify from their characteristic shape (see p. 57). Note that the cast antlers may show signs of gnawing by the deer themselves or by sheep, rabbits and rodents (measure width of incisor marks to establish which).

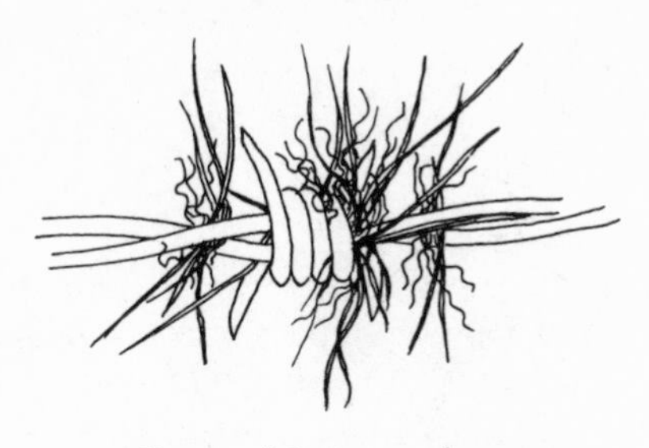

Stiff guard hairs and wavy underhairs snagged on barbed wire.

Hair tufts Fights between males (or a female rebuffing an amorous male) may lead to hair tufts being pulled out among many of the mammal species. This is commonest among deer, rabbits and hares.

Territory disputes between cats can really send the fur flying!

Tufts of hair can also be snagged or pulled out as mammals pass under or over a barbed wire fence or thorny hedge. These can be identified by the detective using the type of hair, its length and colour (see also the forensic chapter). Hair caught on the top strand of a barbed wire fence is likely to be from a horse or a cow, but deer hair is sometimes caught as they leap a fence. Horse hair is typically long, and fairly thick (particularly if from mane or tail), cow hair can be recognized as being short and soft, often matted together like felt. Deer hairs are fairly stiff and straight like bristles with hollow centres. Middle wire strands may snag at the coats of sheep, dog and fox, as do the bottom wires, particularly where animals have passed underneath. Badger, hare and rabbit hair are typically found along these bottom strands. Badger hair is instantly recognized as being stiff and wiry and marked white at the base, dark in the middle and pale at the tapered tip. Rabbit hairs are usually pulled out in tufts of short, soft and fluffy hairs that are grey with a fawn end. Fox, hare and dog hair can look very similar, being a red-brown or grey-brown colour about an inch long (25 mm). Forensic examination is needed to identify these.

To sum up

Marine mammals

Even for the most experienced mammal detective, tracking down the marine mammals represents the ultimate challenge.

The task is made all the more difficult by the fact that the sea is often too rough to allow good visibility whether you are watching from the land or from a boat. Even when glimpsed, the animal in its natural environment is notoriously difficult to identify because distances and the relative size of the whale, dolphin or seal are difficult to judge accurately. It's very much like trying to assess the size of an iceberg, the majority of which is hidden below the water's surface (mind you I don't expect you have seen many icebergs either!). A further problem is that the animals never seem to fit the textbook descriptions since individuals may vary in size and markings and the apparent colouration depends very much on the available light conditions.

Once mastered, however, marine mammal spotting can be very rewarding and productive but be prepared for long hours without seeing anything except seabirds.

If you hope to gain sightings of the cetaceans from land the best places to choose are the headlands that jut out some way into the sea, offshore islands or some

Vagrant seals.

of the deepwater Scottish sea lochs. Your chances are greatly improved however from a boat or a cruise ship a couple of miles offshore. Ferry journeys are always enlivened for the mammal detective by a bit of **whale** and **dolphin** watching. I once saw the huge back of a 20 metre (65 foot) long fin whale surface immediately beside a car ferry crossing the Kilbrannan Sound from Kintyre to the Isle of Arran, Scotland, a journey that took a mere 20 minutes, where most passengers just sat in their cars and missed a once in a lifetime sighting at such close range.

In British waters the best time to look for virtually every one of the recorded species is between April and October and the coast of the Atlantic seaboard offers the best opportunities. A few of the hot-spots now offer whale-watching cruises and dolphin safaris for the really enthusiastic amateur.

Common and **grey seals** have been recorded from virtually every part of the British coast and have even been seen along inland waterways such as in the River Thames above Tower Bridge, London, on the River Ouse in East Anglia, the River Tyne through Newcastle and in Loch Ness. The best populations of common seals occur around the west coast of Scotland with more restricted breeding groups in the estuaries of the Moray Firth, the Tay and the Wash. The best populations of the grey seal occur around the coasts of south-west England, Wales, the outer Hebrides and Northern Isles as well as the Farne Isles, Northumberland.

The best time to see them is while they are at their breeding grounds which is during the summer for the common seal and during the autumn/early winter for the grey seal.

Vagrants could turn up at any time but especially during the late summer when there is dispersal away from their respective breeding grounds.

Predators

This group comprises the terrestrial hunters; although most prey on other mammals or birds, some show a preference for eating invertebrates or fruit at certain times of the year.

The 11 species of this group vary enormously in their appearance, from the tiny sinuous weasel to the heavy lumbering badger. Their similarities lie in the type of teeth they have, all showing enlarged canines and specialized cheek teeth for cutting and shearing.

Being at the top of the food chain, they are not superabundant like some of the smaller herbivores and many are not only rare but highly elusive.

The mammal detective relies heavily on the field signs they leave in order to determine their presence, but because of the similar diet of many of these predators the droppings can be very confusing.

Every mammal detective has a favourite animal; mine has to be the **otter**, since I spent six years carrying out surveys for them along the rivers of England and many more years just looking for them out of personal interest. Yet if I were to add up all my sightings, minute by minute, I would still only have achieved less than two days' worth.

This elusiveness entices the mammal detective. Even those animals that have

An animal glimpsed at dusk - was it an otter?

been the subjects of years of study and understanding somehow still manage to be unpredictable and difficult to track down. It is relatively easy to prove you have an otter around, due to its distinctive spraint, but it is much more difficult to put yourself in the right place at the right time in order to watch it. Nothing is quite so magical as catching a glimpse of an otter fishing just as the sun is setting and a gentle breeze rustles the reeds. I have a few favourite places for otter-watching, but I'm afraid I'll be keeping those to myself. The Scottish islands and sea lochs are good, especially at dawn and dusk, with Shetland perhaps supporting the densest population of otters anywhere in western Europe. In these less disturbed places otters can be active at any time of the day responding to the ebb and flood of the tide; elsewhere they are very wary of man and lead a nocturnal lifestyle.

Best otter-watching conditions are when the water's surface is flat and calm, for then any movement of a swimming animal or its wake can be detected. When the otter is fishing its diving can catch the eye, as the tail is flicked up (at a distance this helps distinguish otter from seal). The dive may last a minute or more and allows time for the observer to try and get a bit closer (the same is true for seals).

Another favourite of mine – but even more elusive – is the enigmatic **pine marten.** This species has suffered badly due to persecution by man and its range has contracted to north-west Scotland and a few remote areas of northern England and Wales. For the mammal detective its presence can be readily determined by its characteristic droppings (and their distinctive odour); obtaining a sighting is a totally different matter. Even researchers following a radio-tracked individual are rarely allowed sightings. This species likes vegetation cover and the cover of darkness. In winter a blanket of lying snow may reveal a good trail of tracks in pairs or groups of four, each showing five toes but appearing indistinct due to the dense fur on the soles (as in rabbits and hares). In order to get close to this species I can only really suggest the western Highlands of Scotland. Here there are a few localities where the marten has been encouraged to the garden bird table and even to take food out of the hand (they seem to have developed a liking for fruitcake, raspberry jam and peanut butter!).

One mustelid that is relatively easy to track down is the **mink**, due to its habit of hunting river margins, leaving behind a set of tracks in the wet silt. Although a relatively new addition to the British list due to escapes from fur farms (mainly in the 1950s and 60s), this species is still increasing its distribution range in Britain and can now be classed as widespread. Favourite den sites include riverside tree roots, pollarded willows and rabbit burrows. Once a den is located (indicated by a pile of droppings near the entrance) regular observation from a suitable vantage point should allow a sighting at dusk. I have watched a mink in broad daylight fishing for crayfish that it hunted by diving among submerged tree roots. It caught three within a ten-minute period, each time bringing the hapless crustacean to the shore to eat with loud crunches.

Rabbit burrows are favoured as dens by the next carnivore, the **polecat**. However, by comparison with the mink, this species is much harder to track down and its field signs are very difficult to distinguish from those of the mink. Most of its scats appear to be left underground in the rabbit burrows where it spends the majority of its time hunting. My own encounters with polecats have only been of dead ones on the road, but these road casualties have confirmed that the species is now spreading back into England from Wales.

Both the **stoat** and the **weasel** are most likely to be seen as a sinuous shape streaking across the road. However, the mammal detective can find tracks and scats of both by searching field boundaries. Drystone walls are particularly good places for weasels as they can dart in and out of the cracks and crevices. At one such site in the Yorkshire Dales I have managed to find the distinctive small and twisted weasel scats on top of the wall beside a gatepost every time I looked. Both stoat and weasel may hunt field boundaries and even across open ground during the daylight, searching for rabbits, rats, mice, voles and small birds. Once you have located a place where the footprints and scats can regularly be found it will only be a matter of time before you are treated to your first prolonged sighting; remember that they are inquisitive and can be called to you by squeaking through wet lips. I was once able to call up a family party of five young weasels to within two metres of me.

Weasels may also be encountered as the unexpected occupants of a Longworth trap or bird box. My most unusual encounter with a stoat, however, was in a farmhouse loft. I had been called to investigate the farm's bats which turned out to be a roost of 60 long-eared bats, but while in the loft I noticed the characteristic scats of a stoat on the rafters and loft insulation. Suddenly a noise at the eaves made me swing around with my torch to catch in the beam of light a stoat carrying a full grown dead rabbit. Not only had the stoat managed to make a regular den in the loft by climbing two storeys up the outside wall, it had managed to drag its prey (more than twice its weight) up there too!

The field signs of the **badger** can be very obvious and distinctive – a well trodden run, its track, dung pits, hair caught on barbed wire and, of course, its sett. The sett can be often found by following the runs the animals use. Badger watching at a sett at dusk is remarkably rewarding as the distinctive black-and-white striped face appears in the fading light, as if on a stage in front of you. A few peanuts scattered around the sett entrances encourage the animals to stay and feed nearby, but remember to keep quiet and watch out for changes in wind direction that may carry your scent to the sett. Always arrive early to settle yourself in place and only leave when the animals have moved off or are unlikely to be frightened by your movement.

The **fox** is common and widespread and it is very easy for the mammal detective to prove their presence since they leave their droppings in prominent places (such as on top of tussocks, molehills or rocks beside a path) and have a very strong and characteristic scent. Their footprints are fairly readily distinguished from those of dogs and the trail is recognized as a single line of tracks. Sightings are best made at dawn and dusk and for me there will always be a magic that surrounds the sight of a fox pouncing on a grass tussock to flush out a field vole in the orange glow of a frosty winter's day-break.

The **wildcat** is now locally confined to a number of Scottish forested hills and is notoriously difficult to track down.

I have only glimpsed one animal that I am convinced was a wildcat. This was at night in the beam of the car headlights as the animal crossed the road beside a small Scottish lochan. Its green eyeshine was first picked out some fifty metres in front of me and as it crossed the big bushy blunt-tipped tail was very obvious; it then jumped up the bank to disappear among heather and pine trees. I stopped and searched the spot where it went and found clear tracks from the jump that measured three metres apart.

Even where this species thrives it is not common and sightings are rare, often being no more than a glimpse of one on a forest track at dawn or dusk. Only a blanket of lying snow may reveal the line of tracks that confirm its presence to the mammal detective.

Browsers and grazers

This group comprises of all the larger herbivores that feed extensively on leaves and grass. It includes the deer, rabbits and hares, feral goats, semi-wild ponies, domestic stock and feral wallabies. Their large size and social behaviour allow the detective to track them down fairly easily and gain good sightings. Their field

The ears and tusks give this one away as a Chinese water deer.

signs are also frequently encountered but because of their similar diet the mammal detective can often be confused over the tracks and droppings left by them.

All of the **deer** species in Britain are primarily woodland animals which like to hide themselves away during the day, venturing out into the open in the twilight of dawn and dusk. This doesn't mean that you will not see them during the day, it's just that they are harder to find even when you know where to look. An exception to this is in the rutting season (at its peak in October), when large herds of red, sika and fallow deer may build up, the stags bellowing (more of a whistling groan in the case of the sika) to proclaim territory and a group of hinds. On the open hillsides of the high mountains of Scotland there is no sound more evocative than a roaring contest of red deer stags, followed by a clash of antlers.

The most widespread of the deer species is the roe and the mammal detective should easily be able to determine its presence in a wood by its tracks, droppings and fraying stocks during its rut (late June to early August, earlier than the larger deer species). Watching woodland edges and rides at either dawn or dusk from a concealed vantage point (or even a deer hide known as a high seat) will allow you to observe roe and other species if present. Alternatively, deer can be stalked on foot by moving slowly below the skyline and using trees as cover, but remember to try and keep the wind in your face or you will soon be scented and all you will see is a fleeing deer's bottom!

Apart from the Scottish Highlands and islands, red deer occur on Exmoor and the Quantocks, New Forest, Thetford and Suffolk coastal woods, parts of Lancashire and Cumbria and a few scattered pockets elsewhere as escapes from deer parks or deer farms. Sika deer are localized to their introduction sites with their strongholds in the Dorset and Hampshire forests as well as parts of Argyll, Inverness and Sutherland in Scotland. Strongholds for the fallow deer are equally localized although more widespread through southern England, south Wales and Scotland.

The muntjac was introduced to Woburn and Whipsnade parks in Bedfordshire in the 1920s, since when it has spread to most of the southern, eastern and midland counties of England. Its tiny hoofprints and small black shiny pellets reveal its presence in a woodland but it is also easy to overlook since it will often sit tight in a bramble patch as you walk past. Once sighted, however, it is possible to stalk to within ten or so metres' range. On one memorable occasion I approached downwind of a muntjac to about six metres and squatted down to observe its browsing with binoculars. To my amazement the tiny deer walked straight towards me to eat a few leaves from the bramble bush beside my legs. It gave a quick sniff at my knees and then casually walked away, pausing briefly to eat another bramble leaf. If only I had had my camera !

Like the muntjac, the Chinese water deer has escaped into the wild from a number of deer parks, but, unlike the muntjac, it has only managed to survive in a few pockets of suitable habitat. The best population is known from Woodwalton Fen in Cambridgeshire. It also occurs elsewhere at other wetland sites in East Anglia, but sightings are difficult due to the nature of the dense vegetation it prefers to hide in.

Feral **goats** occur in small and discrete populations among coastal cliffs, forested hills and mountains of Wales, Scotland and some Scottish islands. This shaggy coated animal with long curving horns is distinctive to look at, but its field signs can often be confused with deer and sheep.

A surprising addition to the list of British browsing animals is the red-necked **wallaby**. The best known feral population occurs in the Peak District derived from an introduction in 1940. Elsewhere escapes from parks and private collections have given rise to reports of these animals in parts of Scotland, northern England (2 were living wild in Durham in 1993) and parts of southern England. Their tracks in snow are unmistakeable, with the hindfoot measuring 20–22cm (7–8 inches), showing a long heel and only two large toes. Their droppings are found as oval pellets left as 5 or 6 in a line, whereas the other browsers all tend to leave their pellet groups as a clump.

Rabbits, brown **hares** and mountain hares are all fairly easy to track down by the mammal detective and the best time to watch, like many of our other mam-

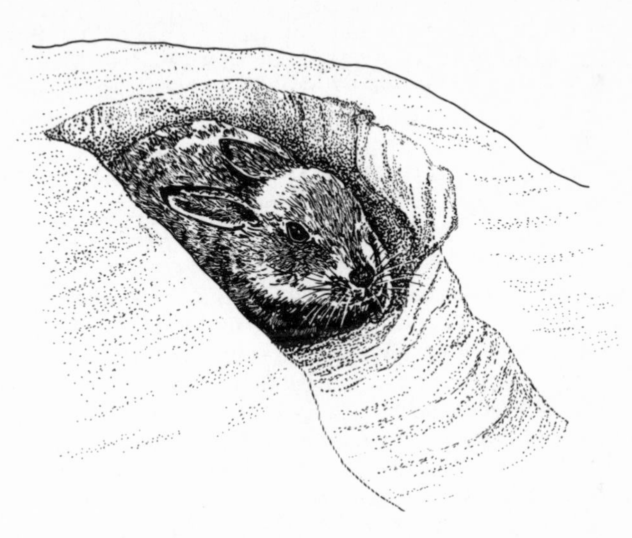

Mountain hare form is dug into snow.

mals, is at dawn or dusk. The antics of 'mad march hares', congregating in the middle of fields to box, chase and court one another is infamous and a joy to watch. Rabbits and brown hares are found throughout Britain, but the mountain hare, as its name suggests, is localized to the Highlands of Scotland, Skye, Mull, Jura and the Scottish southern uplands as well as an introduced population in the Peak District.

Gnawers and nibblers

This group includes all the rodents that are characterized by the pair of enlarged chisel-shaped front teeth, which they use for gnawing and nibbling.

The group includes 2 squirrels, 2 dormice, 2 rats, 4 voles and 4 mice, all of which leave very similar feeding remains, tracks and droppings. All show a 5-toed hind foot and 4-toed fore foot and pellet type droppings but they differ in size depending on species.

For the mammal detective the best way to track down **squirrels** is by looking for their distinctive dreys and feeding remains such as chewed pine cones. If you can hear their food debris falling from the canopy you should soon be treated to a sighting, whether of a red or a grey. The grey squirrel is now very widespread throughout Britain (and still spreading into northern England and parts of Scotland), being most at home in deciduous woodland (and suburban gardens). By contrast the red squirrel is contracting its range and now is best looked for in the extensive forestry plantations of Scotland, northern England and parts of Wales, together with a few population pockets in East Anglia, Isle of Wight and Brownsea Island (Dorset).

Like the red squirrel, the hazel **dormouse** has also contracted its range and is now best looked for in southern England and South Wales (although I do know of one or two outposts for it in northern England). The most characteristic field signs are gouged-out hazelnuts and its nest woven out of stripped honeysuckle bark. Unless accidentally disturbed from its nest during the day, sightings are virtually impossible, due to it being nocturnal and spending all its time hidden among the canopy leaves.

Woodmice and **yellow necked mice** are also mainly nocturnal and, as their names suggest, are most at home under a canopy of trees. They spend a lot of time foraging on the ground but they are also good climbers. The most obvious field signs these animals leave are cached food remains brought to a place of cover such as a tree hollow. Whereas the woodmouse is widespread, the slightly larger yellow-necked mouse is confined to southern England and parts of Wales.

By contrast to woodmice, **voles** are much more likely to be active during the day. Their runs and feeding remains (seeds in the case of bank vole and grass stalks in the case of field vole) can be found by searching the low growing vegetation. Both are widespread in Britain.

Harvest mice have a southern and eastern distribution in Britain (as far north as Yorkshire). They are best located by searching for their distinctive tennis ball-sized nests in the stalk zone of the vegetation. New nests are difficult to spot since they are woven out of living grass leaves, but the task is made much easier in early winter when the withered, brown, grass nest-balls really stand out among the dead grass stalks.

Dormouse nest woven out of honeysuckle bark.

The widespread **house mouse** can be encountered in most habitats but it is most frequently found around buildings and food stores like its bigger cousin the **brown rat.** By contrast the black rat has virtually disappeared from Britain and is now only found at a few coastal ports and docks, and on the island of Lundy in the Bristol Channel.

In recent years the formerly widespread **water vole** has become much scarcer along Britain's waterways. Its presence is best determined by searching for its burrows, latrines (piles of distinctive droppings) and feeding remains. This species can easily be observed by patiently waiting by the riverbank once its field signs have been located, since it can be active throughout the day. There is something really rewarding about being able to sit quietly on a riverbank on a warm summer's day, just watching water voles swim about, felling reed stems like mini lumberjacks and then dragging the stems to a favoured platform where they will sit on their haunches to chew the ends. Watching the young ones out on their first exploratory excursions, bobbing about like corks, are moments never to be forgotten.

Insect crunchers

This group includes the hedgehog, mole, the shrews and the bats and only the latter two groups may cause problems of identification and determining which species are present.

Hedgehogs are one of the few British wild mammals that you can watch at really close range, going about their normal business of snuffling up slugs, snails, worms and insects. This does mean, however, that you must be prepared to go out looking for them at night (or wait until their nightly foraging brings them into your garden). As most gardeners will know, the proof that you have had a visitation by a hedgehog is its distinctive droppings on the lawn. The other field sign that the mammal detective may like to look for is its nest, which is usually in a dry place, built out of vegetation (fallen twigs, leaves and grasses) and has ground level access (such as under a shed or in a dense hedge).

Moles are easy to detect due to their very obvious 'molehills', but obtaining a sighting of one can be very frustrating since they rarely come out of their tunnels and only a pink nose may be seen as the soil mound is being created. The best opportunities to observe moles are when they are digging on the surface in the leaf litter of woodlands. By quietly standing still and watching, the mole may be seen from time to time beneath the heaving leaves as it extends its burrows and hunts for worms.

Although the **shrews** probably are some of Britain's most widespread and abundant mammals, they, like the mole, are rarely seen because they spend three-quarters of their time underground or in dense vegetation. Often the only sign that they are nearby comes from their distinctive shrill squeaking and scurrying sounds from the undergrowth. On hearing such calls, a bit of patient waiting and watching may allow some interesting observations to be made of territorial disputes or family group interaction. I once heard a shrill squeaking that I initially mistook for that of noctule bats and was looking around and up at the trees for a suitable hole when I realized the sound originated from a clump of sedge beside a pool. Suddenly six tiny black and grey bodies burst out in all directions from the sedge to hurtle across the water's surface at frantic speed, their tiny legs whirring like clockwork, each animal giving the appearance of walking on water. They were of course water shrews.

Most people's encounters with **bats** are as shadowy figures in flight at dusk when it is difficult to judge size. The only safe way to positively identify a bat is by examination in the hand (which requires a licence) however, there are certain factors that help identify bats in flight and these are:

1 Time of emergence in relation to sunset; for instance, noctules and pipistrelles come out as the sun is setting but Natterer's and long-eareds wait until total darkness.

2 Apparent size and the way the wings appear to beat: noctules and Leisler's have long narrow wings and tend to fly with fast beats high above the tree tops, whereas the equally large but broad winged greater horseshoe has a fluttery flight around bushes and tree canopies, while the medium-sized Daubenton's skim close over a water's surface with shallow wing beats like mini hovercraft.

3 Converted ultrasounds using a bat detector: each of the different bat species produces a discernible pattern of ultrasound pulses (above that of human hearing) that can be heard as clicks, slaps or warbles on the bat detector. Different bats may be listened for at different frequencies by tuning the detector; for instance, the lesser horseshoe is best heard at 105 kHz, the greater horseshoe at 80 kHz while the noctule at 20 kHz (see Identity parade information on pp. 72-4).

The bat detector has provided a real advance in the study of bats but confident identification still requires considerable practice and experience.

Proving the presence of bats through detective work can help conserve this endangered group of mammals. Much of the work of licensed bat enthusiasts involves surveys of loft spaces and roofs for bat signs, prior to proposed remedial timber treatment against woodworm or rot so that advice can be given on the types of chemicals used and the timing of spraying. This must have saved thousands of bats from being unintentionally poisoned, especially when the animals themselves may have been tucked away out of sight (but the droppings had been spotted by the batworker). Similarly by tracking back the flight paths of bats to buildings, bridges, tunnels, caves or trees, batworkers have been able to save or secure these valuable roost sites and even the flyways used by the bats in some cases. These are a few of the mammal detective skills currently being used to actively conserve this delightful group of animals. By joining your local bat group you too can bring your skills into effective use.

The mammal detective's library

The quest for knowledge drives the mammal detective, his or her enquiring mind always posing more and more questions until it can be finally said, 'Ah, so that's what it is !' or 'Oh, so that's why, that's what it is all about !'

To this end the complete mammal detective always has an extensive collection of reference books. As I look around my library of mammal books, I see a whole range of useful material from general textbooks, to species monographs and specialist identification keys.

Below I have listed a few that are musts for every mammal detective and a few others that can be used to dip into from time to time. Some provide the most up to date information from the recent research on a particular species, or have particularly good illustrations, while a few are just a thoroughly good read and are a joy to have.

Essential references

The Handbook of British Mammals edited by Gordon Corbet and Stephen Harris (3rd edition, Blackwell Scientific Publications, Oxford, 1991). A mine of information and a Bible for the mammal detective.

Atlas of British Mammals by Henry Arnold (Biological Records Centre, Monks Wood, Huntingdon, 1993)

Mammal Watching by Michael Clark (Severn House Publishers Ltd, London, 1981)

Mammals of Britain their tracks, trails and signs by M. J. Lawrence & R. W. Brown (Blandford Press Ltd, London, 1967)

Animal Tracks and Signs by P. Bang & P. Dahlstrom (Collins, Glasgow, 1974)

Observing British and European Mammals by C. Bouchardy & F. Moutou (British Museum (Natural History), London, 1989)

Recommended specialist books

Hair of West European mammals: Atlas and Identification by B. J. Teerink (Cambridge University Press, Cambridge, 1991)

The Analysis of Owl Pellets by D. W. Yalden, & P. A. Morris (Occasional Publication of The Mammal Society, No.13. Mammal Society, London, 1990)

Owls and bone cave deposits by P. Andrews (British Museum (Natural History), London, 1991)

A guide to the identification of prey remains in Otter Spraint by J. Conroy, J. Watt, J. Webb & A. Jones (Occasional publication of the Mammal Society, No.16. Mammal Society, London 1993)

The Analysis of Bat Droppings by C. McAney, C. Shiel, C. Sullivan & J. Fairley (Occasional publication of the Mammal Society, No.14 Mammal Society, London 1992)

Live Trapping Small Mammals - a practical guide by J. Gurnell and J. R. Flowerdew (occasional publication of the Mammal Society, No.3. Mammal Society, London 1990)

Wildlife Radio Tagging: equipment, field techniques and data analysis by R. Kenward (Academic Press, London, 1987)

A Guide to Bats of Britain and Europe by W. Schrober and E. Grimmberger (consultant editor R.E. Stebbings) (Hamlyn, London, 1989).

Species monographs

Christopher Helm Mammal Series: *The Natural History of Badgers, Otters, Squirrels, Deer, Moles, Shrews, Hibernating Bats, Weasels and Stoats, Seals, Whales and Dolphins.*

Whittet monographs on *Badgers, Bats, Deer, Hedgehogs, Mice and Voles, Otters, Ponies in the Wild, Rabbits and Hares, Seals, Squirrels, Stoats and Weasels, Polecats and Martens, Urban Foxes, Whales* and *Wildcats*

Useful addresses

The Mammal Society, Unit 15 Cloisters House, Cloisters Business Centre, 8 Battersea Park Road, London SW8 4BG

Bat Conservation Trust, c/o London Ecology Centre, 45 Shelton St, London WC2H 9HJ

Biological Records Centre, Monks Wood Experimental Station, Abbots Ripton, Huntingdon PE17 2LS

County Wildlife Trusts (addresses in local telephone directories or from libraries)

Statutory Nature Conservation Organizations (SNCOs):

For England – English Nature, Northminster House, Peterborough PE1 1UA

For Scotland – Scottish Natural Heritage, 12 Hope Terrace, Edinburgh EH9 2AS

For Wales – Countryside Council for Wales, Plas Penrhos, Ffordd Penrhos, Bangor, Gwynedd LL57 2LQ

Suppliers

Longworth small mammal traps

Penlon Ltd, Radley Road, Abingdon, Oxon OX14 3PH

The living trip-trap

North West Plastics Ltd, Worsley, Manchester M28 4AJ

(transparent sides allow you to see what has been caught !)

The Mammal Society trap loan scheme (members can hire up to 10 or more Longworth traps for periods of up to 35 days) from:

H.W. Pepper, Wildlife Conservation Research Branch, Forest Research Station, Alice Holt Lodge, Wrecclesham, Surrey GU10 4LH.

Bat detectors

Bat Box III

Stag Electronics, 1 Rosemundy, St Agnes, Cornwall TR5 0UF

Mini-2 Bat detector

Summit, 74 Wheeleys Road, Birmingham B15 2LN

Skye Ultrasonic Receiver: Skye Instruments Ltd, Unit 6 Dhole Industrial Estate, Llandrindod Wells, Powys LD1 6DF

Index